FEED THE FUTURE

The U.S. Government's Global Hunger & Food Security Initiative

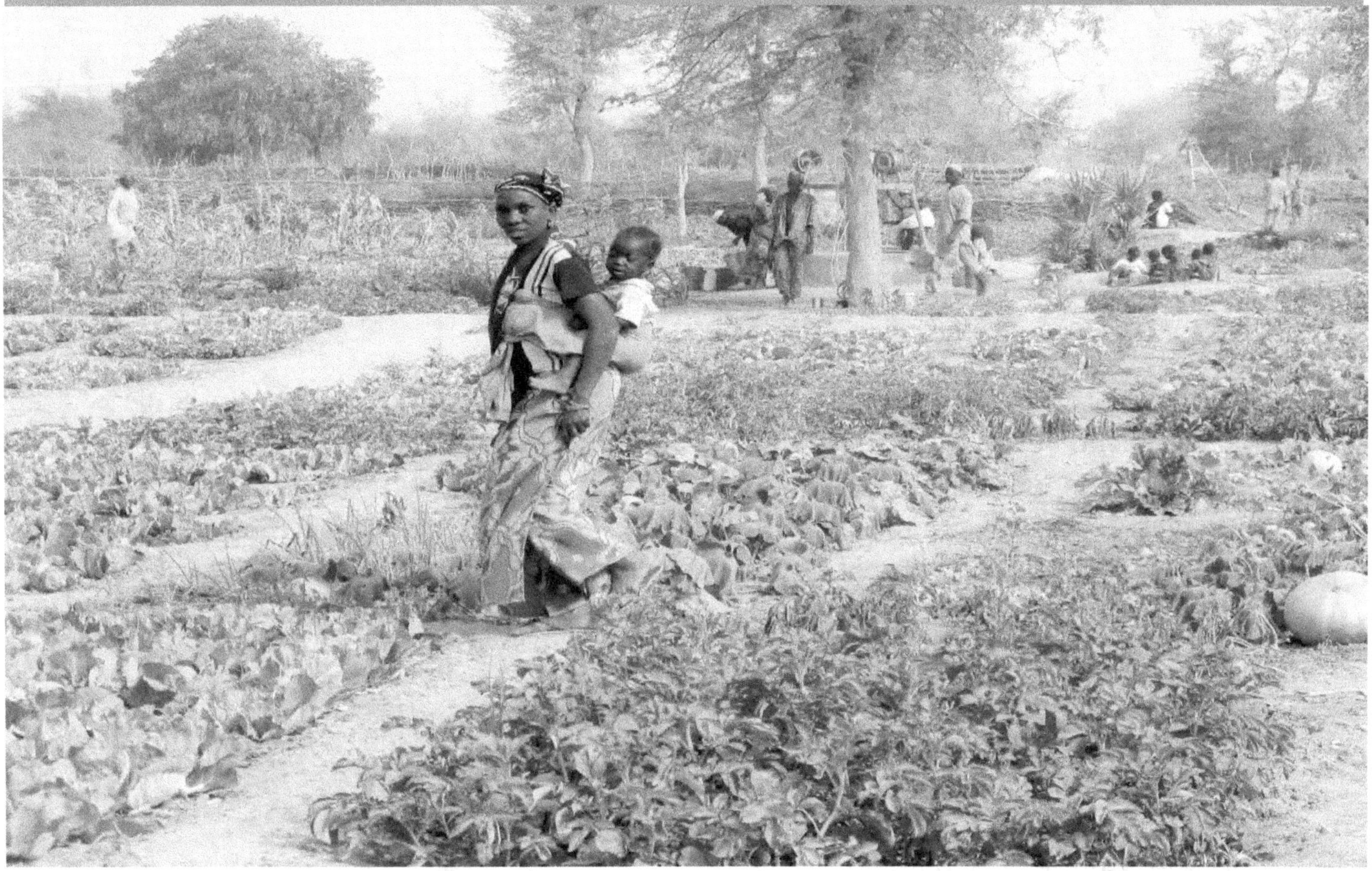

Feed the Future Global Performance Evaluation
Final Evaluation Report Annexes
December 2016

FROM THE AMERICAN PEOPLE

Prepared for the United States Agency for International Development under USAID Contract Number AID-OAA-I-15-00019/ AID-OAA-TO-16-00003. This publication was prepared independently by: Lee Briggs, Evaluation Team Leader; Patricia Vondal, Senior Evaluation Specialist; Charu Vijayakumar, Evaluation Specialist; Michael Maxey, Senior Technical Advisor; Allyson Bear, Senior Technical Advisor; Derek Byerlee, Senior Research Advisor; Lauren Rosapep, Evaluation Specialist; Amun Nadeem, Evaluation Specialist; and William Fiebig, Senior Technical Advisor

USAID/Bureau for Food Security (BFS) Contact:
ehogue@usaid.gov

Dexis Consulting Group Contact:
1412 I St. NW, Washington, DC, 20009
202-625-9444
contracts@dexisonline.com

TABLE OF CONTENTS

ANNEX I: EVALUATION STATEMENT OF WORK

Scope and Objectives

This evaluation is of Feed the Future, as a whole, with a special emphasis on the 19 focus countries and ZOIs where Feed the Future activities have been operating intensively. Of the 19 Feed the Future Focus Countries, four to five countries will be chosen by the evaluation team in consultation with the Feed the Future Internal Evaluation Panel (see Section 6) for in-depth evaluation. Additionally, the evaluation will include the regional programs (especially the three African regional programs) along with BFS programs including Agricultural Research; Agricultural Policy; Markets, Partnerships, and Innovations; and Monitoring, Evaluation and Learning (MEL). The range of programs to be evaluated includes those programs or interventions for which results are entered into the FTFMS. Within USAID, those activities reporting into FTFMS include those supported by the following funding streams: agriculture (including nutrition sensitive agriculture, market development, agricultural-linked trade promotion) through approximately $1 billion appropriated annually to USAID for Feed the Future; Food for Peace (FFP) development programs worldwide, of which Feed the Future funds approximately 20 percent through Community Development Funds; and nutrition-focused activities funded through the global health account. For FFP development and Global Health nutrition funding, the focus will be on how they contribute to Feed the Future's impact in the 19 zones of influence.

According to USAID, "[p]erformance evaluations represent a broad range of evaluation methods. They often incorporate before-after comparisons, but generally lack a rigorously defined counterfactual. Performance evaluations focus on what a particular project or program has achieved; how it was implemented; how it was perceived and valued; whether expected results occurred; and other questions that are pertinent to project design, management and operational decision making." (USAID Evaluation Toolkit: Guidance, Tools, and Resources for Planning, Managing and Learning from Evaluations, April 2015, p. 7). In this case, the evaluation will provide a large-scale evaluation of a complex initiative targeting food security, agricultural development, nutrition and related services.

The scope of the evaluation, or programs to be evaluated, is further specified as:
   a. Examine performance across the entire initiative, with an emphasis on performance in Focus Countries. Use the Feed the Future Guide and any identified follow-on guidance provided by BFS as a framework to define the initiative and to determine the breadth of programs to be evaluated, and address the questions outlined above.
   b. Examine performance of Feed the Future programs in-country for Feed the Future Focus, Aligned, and Regional Missions, with an emphasis on Focus Countries.

    i.   Broadly assess performance in the 19 Focus Countries remotely, via document and data reviews, phone interviews, and email interviews or surveys.

    ii.   Conduct in-depth assessments on the ground within four to five of the Feed the Future Focus Countries selecting sample countries in coordination with the IEP.

    iii.   Assess a subset of the Aligned Countries remotely, via document and data reviews, phone interviews, and email interviews or surveys.

    iv.   Assess the five regional programs remotely via document and data review, phone, and email, with an emphasis on the three African regional Missions.

c. Assess the performance of BFS-managed programs related to Agricultural Research; Agricultural and Nutrition Policy and Enabling Environment; the Market and Partnership Innovations; and Monitoring, Evaluation, and Learning.

d. Examine the overall effectiveness of USAID and BFS in leading the initiative and the effectiveness of the inter-agency process.

e. The Evaluation will rely on a series of systematic interviews with representatives of the variety of organizations and institutions described above, including implementing partners and partner government agencies. Interviews may be supplemented by e-mail and telephone surveys.

The evaluation will employ appropriate qualitative and quantitative social science research methodologies. Potential qualitative methods to be used are interviews, focus groups, surveys, document review, and direct observation. Potential quantitative methods would include analysis of secondary sources of quantitative data, such as Feed the Future population-based surveys, annual reporting data in the FTFMS, activity performance reports and external evaluation reports of Feed the Future activities. It is not anticipated that primary quantitative data will be collected for this evaluation.

To ensure a strong methodological approach, the evaluation design should consider the context within which Feed the Future is operating and evolving.

- Appreciate the views of the Feed the Future Focus Country government counterparts and those involved in their multi-stakeholder platforms.
- Incorporate the perspectives of the various U.S. Government agency partners working on FTF, to include: USAID (Bureau for Food Security, Food for Peace, regional bureaus, etc.); U.S. Departments of Agriculture, Treasury, State and Commerce, the Millennium Challenge Corporation; Peace Corps, , the U.S. African Development Foundation, Overseas Private Investment Corporation, U.S.T.R. and the White House's Office of Management and Budget.
- Appreciate the views of those organizations that are not directly involved in the initiative through a formalized partnership (signed Memorandum of Understanding or

similar agreement) or by receiving Feed the Future funding. This should include civil society, business, and development partners.

- Consider that Feed the Future activities and results are built on the Initiative to End Hunger in Africa (IEHA) and the Global Food Security Response (GFSR), two predecessor food security initiatives from which Feed the Future results really cannot be completely disconnected--particularly in relation to activities related to agricultural research and development--and take interdependence into account in the evaluation methodology and the final report.
- Anticipate the future direction of the initiative.

Data sources will include Feed the Future Focus Country project and program data posted in the FTFMS as well as materials on Feed the Future that are pertinent to the evaluation, to include: a) The Feed the Future Guide, b) The Feed the Future Progress Reports for 2012 to 2015, c) The Feed the Future Research Agenda, and d) The Feed the Future Learning Agenda.

Illustrative focus country data sources include but are not limited to:

a. FTF/Country Multi-Year Strategy (MYSes)
b. Country Investment Plans (CIPs)
c. Annual Feed the Future Portfolio Reviews
d. Annual BFS Portfolio Reviews
e. Program descriptions and statements of work
f. Activity monitoring and evaluation plans
g. Feed the Future performance management plans
h. Project and activity performance and impact evaluation reports
i. Activity quarterly and annual reports
j. Activity data quality assessment reports
k. Feed the Future baseline data from primary and secondary sources
l. Activity baseline survey reports and beneficiary surveys
m. Cost benefit analyses of Feed the Future programs
n. Comprehensive Food Security and Vulnerability Assessments (CFSVA)
o. Gender Assessment for the USAID/Country CDCS
p. Country Demographic and Health Surveys Reports
q. Country National Panel Surveys Reports
r. Country Household Budget Surveys Reports
s. Feed the Future Policy Matrices and Summaries and Interagency Feed the Future Policy Guide
t. New Alliance Cooperation Frameworks and Annual Reports
u. Regional Strategic Analysis and Knowledge Support Systems reports and website

The Strategic Planning and Performance Management (SPPM) Office in BFS provides support in the areas of Budgeting, Monitoring, Evaluation, and Learning to BFS and USAID missions that are programming foreign assistance in agriculture and food security. The SPPM Office will provide documents for the desk review, as well as contact information for prospective interviewees to be selected by the evaluation team. The evaluation team will be responsible for identifying and reviewing additional materials relevant to the evaluation, as well as additional contacts.

2) Evaluation Questions

The evaluation will collect and analyze data to answer the following questions on the performance of the Feed the Future initiative.

Assess the Feed the Future initiative's progress against its strategic goals and objectives in the field of operation, including:

a. Adherence to and progress across the Feed the Future Results Framework across the initiative. How well have strategies and the implementation of programs followed the Results Framework and the causal pathways identified therein?

b. How has the Feed the Future initiative performed against each of its eight intermediate results outlined in the Results Framework across focus countries? Does the progress made against the eight Intermediate Results to date, coupled with changes in impact-level indicators, provide evidence that Feed the Future is on track to achieve its five-year goals of reducing poverty and stunting by 20 percent?

c. The implementation and effectiveness of the "selectivity and focus" approach within given country or regional portfolios.

   i. How well has Feed the Future focused resources on strategic and limited value chains? How have value chain approaches been applied and what have been the successes and challenges to these approaches?

   ii. How well has the initiative focused implementation and concentrated resources in appropriate (in terms of size and agro-ecology) geographic zones? What have been successful strategies, if any?

   iii. To what extent has Feed the Future scaled up agriculture and nutrition interventions across the ZOI in Feed the Future Focus Countries? Are the proportions of households being reached in each ZOI sufficient to plausibly achieve the targeted impacts?

d. How and to what extent have Feed the Future interventions, both Mission- and centrally-managed, helped build human and institutional capacities for the agricultural and nutrition/health sectors?

e. How and to what extent have Feed the Future interventions promoted gender-inclusive agricultural sector growth and improved nutritional status of women through equitable and strategic integration of women and men in agriculture and nutrition programs?

f. How well have Feed the Future interventions integrated nutrition into value chain activities? Do results differ if nutrition objectives are an integral part of the value chain work? If so, how?

Using the Feed the Future Guide as a reference point, assess the performance and management of the Feed the Future initiative as a whole, specifically in terms of relevance, efficiency, effectiveness, and sustainability. Key questions include:

a. The effectiveness of the initiative's focus on country ownership. How well has Feed the Future invested in country-owned plans that support results-based programs and partnerships?

b. What has been Feed the Future's contribution to influencing and leveraging multi-lateral institutions and initiatives, thus shaping the evolving food security landscape, which will, in turn, affect the future form and function of the initiative? This includes, but is not limited to: i) the G8 and the New Alliance; ii) the Comprehensive Africa Agriculture Development Program (CAADP); iii) the Global Agriculture and Food Security Program (GAFSP); iv) the Consultative Group for International Agricultural Research ;v) Monitoring and Evaluation frameworks for food security programs; vi) in-country agriculture or nutrition information systems.

c. The effectiveness, relevance, and collaboration in FTF's implementation of its research strategy. How effectively is Feed the Future marshaling relevant capacities in U.S. and global research organizations? How well are Feed the Future -supported research activities designed to address major global challenges and spur agricultural development across initiative Focus Countries? To what extent are research products being disseminated and/or commercialized?

d. The Feed the Future initiative's role, both globally and at the country level, in leveraging and increasing private sector participation and funding. How well has the initiative leveraged private sector participation to support agricultural and nutritional outcomes?

e. How well is Feed the Future identifying and promoting policy reform at the national and regional level, including implementation of policy reform? Which kinds of regional policy interventions have been the most effective at contributing to bilateral impacts and why?

f. How well has Feed the Future's system and approaches for monitoring, evaluation, and learning (MEL) facilitated requisite levels of accountability and learning? How well have Feed the Future MEL approaches achieved accountability for commitments Feed the Future has made? Has Feed the Future MEL supported improved programming and how?

3) Oversight of the Evaluation and Assurance of Objectivity and Accuracy

Due to the magnitude and importance of this evaluation, special oversight and support functions will be added to increase the objectivity and accuracy of the evaluation. To that purpose, two bodies will be established and integrated into the evaluation process.

First, an external Evaluation Oversight Committee (EOC) will be created to oversee the conduct of the evaluation and provide input at various points during the evaluation as detailed below in sections F.5. The EOC will consist of international experts from other donor, academic, business, non-governmental, or multi-lateral organizations working in the food security sector. Feed the Future/USAID will select three to five organizations and each organization will appoint one representative to participate on the EOC. The main purpose of the EOC is to ensure the evaluation is conducted in the most objective and transparent way possible, but it will also add a layer of technical oversight, providing recommendations on possible gaps or misdirection in the evaluation.

Second, a Feed the Future Internal Evaluation Panel (IEP) will be established by Feed the Future senior leadership to provide support and direction to the evaluation team as to the design and conduct of the evaluation and the writing of the evaluation report. The IEP will consist of no more than five USG staff working on Feed the Future that represent the various facets of Feed the Future's implementation. The main purpose of the IEP is to ensure the evaluation is accurate and appropriately focused. To that end, the IEP will ensure the evaluation team has clear direction on the evaluation, develops an appropriate evaluation design, has access to the resources it needs, correctly adheres to the evaluation design, and addresses the evaluation questions and scope of the evaluation in the final report.

Management and Staffing – Offeror's overall project team shall be appropriate in size, composition, and skillset to complete the requirements of this RFTOP and meet the educational and experience requirements set forth in both this RFTOP and the IDIQ. Additionally, each team member shall coincide with an established labor category of the IDIQ.

Gender – Women play a critical role in agriculture in Feed the Future Focus countries. Yet their access to, and control over, agricultural inputs and outputs is usually severely limited. Thus women are a main focus of Feed the Future activities, and Feed the Future programs are geared towards the achievement of gender equality, and the empowerment of women. To measure and address the constraints women face in the agricultural sector and improve gender integration in initiative programming, Feed the Future developed the Women's Empowerment in Agriculture Index (WEAI). The contractor will look for appropriate ways to use and promote data from the WEAI in performance evaluations, impact evaluations, and population-based surveys.

The Contractor's work must be in compliance with USAID's Gender Equality and Women's Empowerment Policy. Addressing gender in all USAID activities is a mandatory requirement as a crosscutting theme built into all activities. The Contractor must examine, and analyze gender-related issues in assessing Feed the Future activities.

1. Project Information

a. Feed the Future Background

Feed the Future (FTF) is a Presidential Initiative designed in 2009 and is the U.S. Government's contribution to the intensified global effort focused on reducing high rates of hunger and poverty around the world. This effort is based on a common framework developed as an outcome of the 2009 G8 and G20 Summits for coordinated and comprehensive action among national governments, international donors, civil society, private sector, and other stakeholders. The approach is based on five principles first articulated at the G8 Summit in L'Aquila, Italy, in 2009, which embrace and support the Paris Declaration on Aid Effectiveness and the Accra Agenda for Action. These principles were endorsed unanimously at the 2009 World Summit on Food Security, and became known as the Rome Principles of Sustainable Food Security by 193 countries. The five principles, meant to accelerate progress toward the Millennium Development Goals (MGDs) of halving the proportions of people living in extreme poverty and hunger by 2015 include: 1) investment in country-owned plans that support results based programs and partnerships; 2) strengthen strategic coordination; 3) ensure a comprehensive approach; 4) leverage the benefits of multilateral institutions; and, 5) deliver on sustained and accountable commitments.

FTF was designed as a whole of government (WOG) approach led and coordinated by the U.S. Agency for International Development (USAID) as the locus of international development expertise. Feed the Future encompasses the work of 10 U.S. Government agencies. Of these, the 6 agencies that support field activities provide data on the initiative's annual results: these are USAID, the U. S. Department of Agriculture (USDA), the Millennium Challenge Corporation (MCC), Peace Corps, the Department of the Treasury, and the African Development Foundation. The Department of State and the Office of the United States Trade Representatives help foster major policy changes that support global and local food security.

The initiative was designed to, over five years, sustainably reduce the prevalence of poverty and stunting in children under five years of age by 20% in Feed the Future targeted zones of influence (ZOI) by tackling root causes and employing proven strategies for achieving large scale and lasting impact. Feed the Future is implemented in 19 focus countries, six regionally-based country programs, and various aligned countries.

Focus Countries

19 "focus countries" were selected based on levels of hunger and poverty in rural communities, potential for rapid and sustainable agricultural-led growth, commitment to invest in food security,

opportunities for partnership, and regional synergies. The 19 focus countries include Bangladesh, Cambodia, Ethiopia, Ghana, Guatemala, Haiti, Honduras, Kenya, Liberia, Malawi, Mali, Mozambique, Nepal, Rwanda, Senegal, Tajikistan, Tanzania, Uganda, and Zambia.

Regional Programs

Feed the Future invests in regional organizations and institutions to address significant challenges to food security that are regional in nature through USAID's regional missions in Asia, Central America and Mexico, East Africa, Southern Africa, and the Sahel and West Africa. In Africa, regional organizations include the Southern African Development Community (SADC), the Economic Community of West African States (ECOWAS), and the Common Market for Eastern and Southern Africa (COMESA). Feed the Future also works with the Inter-American Institute for Cooperation on Agriculture and the Asian Development Bank.

Aligned Countries

Feed the Future provides funding to a number of countries to support much-needed agricultural development activities where progress is critical to achieving core U.S. development and foreign policy objectives. FTF refers to those as "aligned countries." Aligned countries share many Feed the Future objectives in their approach to combating hunger, but usually do not have a focused zone of influence (ZOI) and do not report on the impact and high-level outcome indicators outlined by the Feed the Future results framework (RF) because they do not conduct population-based surveys. The aligned countries can change from year to year, and in 2014, Feed the Future aligned countries included: Burma, Democratic Republic of the Congo, Egypt, Georgia, Kyrgyz Republic, Lebanon, Nigeria, South Sudan, Timor-Leste, Yemen, and Zimbabwe.

b. Theory of Change

The Feed the Future Global Initiative strategy is based on an assessment of the drivers of food insecurity, poverty, and malnourishment in developing countries around the world where poverty and malnutrition levels are the highest. The primary strategy to reduce poverty, particularly among populations whose living is derived from the agriculture sector, is to promote inclusive agriculture sector growth in which women, men, youth, and children benefit in terms of jobs and increased household income. The primary strategy to reduce hunger and malnutrition is to promote improved nutritional status, especially for women of reproductive age and children ages five and under. The Feed the Future RF depicts the theory of change through a hierarchy of results that represent the causal pathways to achieve reductions in poverty and hunger (see Illustration 1, on next page).

Specifically, if achievements are made that result in improved agricultural productivity (IR 1), expansion of markets and trade (IR 2), increased investment in agriculture and nutrition-related activities (IR 3), and increased employment opportunities in selected value chains (IR 4), then inclusive agriculture sector growth will increase over time to meet poverty reduction goals. The achievement of each IR is predicated on improvements related to the enabling environment, market efficiency, the development and application of productivity enhancement technologies and agricultural management practices, improvements in internal, cross border, regional, and international agricultural trade, and other key areas critical to higher order outcomes expressed through IRs 1-4. Early on, the Feed the Future initiative adopted a stronger focus on strategies to promote inclusive agricultural growth through the addition of activities to ensure that both women and men benefit by having equal access and opportunities to receive training, to find employment through value chain development activities, to adopt enhanced technologies and management practices, and to attain property rights for land and key productive assets.

The theory of change to improve nutritional status, especially of women and children, is based on evidence that if individuals have improved access to diverse and quality foods (IR 6), adopt improved nutrition-related behaviors (IR 7), and increase use of maternal and child health and nutrition services (IR 8), then nutritional status will improve. There is a synergistic effect between the strategies to achieve inclusive agriculture sector growth and improved nutrition status. With progress in the expansion of markets and trade, and improved agricultural productivity, there will be greater access to diverse and nutritional food. Similarly, with increased incomes and jobs that come from inclusive agriculture sector growth, households can afford to purchase food and to access maternal and child health and nutrition services.

Incorporated in the overall Feed the Future strategy is a set of activities designed to promote increased resiliency of vulnerable communities and households (IR 5) in response to natural and man-made disasters such as prolonged droughts, extreme flooding, and disease outbreaks. Activities include the promotion of "climate smart" agricultural strategies to adapt to global climate change effects in their specific localities, diversification of agriculture related income-generating activities, and access to jobs generated by agriculture sector growth.

Illustration 1: Feed the Future Results Framework

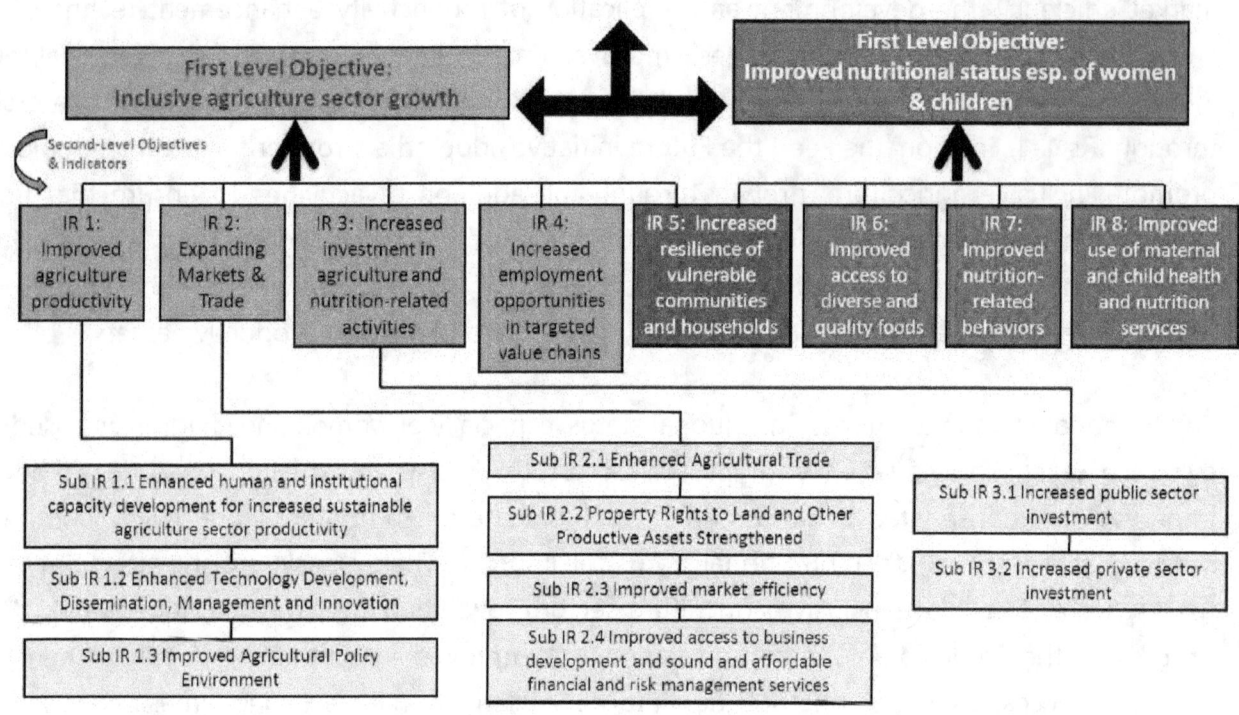

Feed the Future Goal: Sustainably Reduce Global Poverty and Hunger

First Level Objective: Inclusive agriculture sector growth

First Level Objective: Improved nutritional status esp. of women & children

Second-Level Objectives & Indicators

IR 1: Improved agriculture productivity

IR 2: Expanding Markets & Trade

IR 3: Increased investment in agriculture and nutrition-related activities

IR 4: Increased employment opportunities in targeted value chains

IR 5: Increased resilience of vulnerable communities and households

IR 6: Improved access to diverse and quality foods

IR 7: Improved nutrition-related behaviors

IR 8: Improved use of maternal and child health and nutrition services

Sub IR 1.1 Enhanced human and institutional capacity development for increased sustainable agriculture sector productivity

Sub IR 1.2 Enhanced Technology Development, Dissemination, Management and Innovation

Sub IR 1.3 Improved Agricultural Policy Environment

Sub IR 2.1 Enhanced Agricultural Trade

Sub IR 2.2 Property Rights to Land and Other Productive Assets Strengthened

Sub IR 2.3 Improved market efficiency

Sub IR 2.4 Improved access to business development and sound and affordable financial and risk management services

Sub IR 3.1 Increased public sector investment

Sub IR 3.2 Increased private sector investment

2. Evaluation Approach

a. Evaluation Purpose

This is a Performance Evaluation intended to answer questions regarding what Feed the Future has achieved to date, how it is being implemented, and whether expected results are occurring. This is not an impact evaluation and does not have a counterfactual. However, the evaluation will seek to assess the extent to which the initiative has contributed to impacts and results related to reducing poverty, hunger, and under-nutrition, particularly against initiative targets of reducing poverty and stunting by 20 percent.

This evaluation will provide a summative and formative assessment of the Feed the Future initiative's progress for the purposes of accountability and learning, including providing recommendations for future improvements to the initiative. The evaluation will assemble and analyze quantitative and qualitative evidence of the effectiveness and progress to date of the processes, implementation actions, and intermediate results across the initiative leading to reductions in poverty, hunger, and malnutrition.

Understanding how Feed the Future programs are functioning, whether they are achieving targeted results in their focus communities, and whether Feed the Future approaches are scaling-up across broader regions and communities to achieve the high-level Feed the Future goals of sustainably reducing global poverty and hunger is essential for the quality and success of Feed the Future programming. Such knowledge will strengthen accountability, shape resource allocation decisions, foster learning, and allow Feed the Future operating units and implementing partners to modify projects and activities in ways that bolster efficiency and effectiveness.

The scope of coverage for this evaluation will predominantly be the 19 focus countries. However, certain evaluation questions will require the addition of aligned countries and the regional programs.

The evaluation period of performance goes January through December 2016.

b. Evaluation Research Questions

The evaluation research questions are as follows:

Assess the Feed the Future initiative's progress against its strategic goals and objectives in the field of operation, including:

1. Adherence to and progress across the Feed the Future Results Framework across the initiative. How well have strategies and the implementation of programs followed the Results Framework and the causal pathways identified therein?

2. How has the Feed the Future initiative performed against each of its eight intermediate results outlined in the Results Framework across focus countries? Does the progress made against the eight Intermediate Results to date, coupled with changes in impact-level indicators, provide evidence that Feed the Future is on track to achieve its five-year goals of contributing to reductions of 20% in poverty and stunting?

3. The implementation and effectiveness of the "selectivity and focus" approach within given country or regional portfolios.

    a. How have value chain approaches been applied and what have been the successes and challenges to focusing resources on strategic and limited value chains?

    b. How well has the initiative focused implementation and concentrated resources in appropriate (in terms of size and agro-ecology) geographic zones?

    c. Are the proportions of households being reached in the ZOI sufficient to plausibly achieve the targeted impacts?

4. How and to what extent have Feed the Future interventions, both Mission- and centrally-managed, helped build human and institutional capacities for the agricultural and nutrition/health sectors?

5. How and to what extent have Feed the Future interventions promoted gender-inclusive agricultural sector growth and improved nutritional status of women through equitable and strategic integration of women and men in agriculture and nutrition programs?

6. How well have Feed the Future interventions integrated nutrition into value chain activities? Do results differ if nutrition objectives are an integral part of the value chain work? If so, how?

Using the Feed the Future Guide as a reference point, assess the performance and management of the Feed the Future initiative as a whole, specifically in terms of relevance, efficiency, effectiveness, and sustainability. Key questions include:

7. The effectiveness of the initiative's focus on country ownership. How well has Feed the Future fostered country ownership of the Feed the Future program in Focus Countries to support sustainability of outcomes?

8. What has been Feed the Future's contribution to influencing and leveraging multi-lateral institutions and initiatives, specifically i) the G8 and the New Alliance; ii) the Comprehensive Africa Agriculture Development Program (CAADP); iii) the Global Agriculture and Food Security Program (GAFSP); and, iv) the Consultative Group for International Agricultural Research?

9. The effectiveness, relevance, and collaboration in Feed the Future's implementation of its research strategy. How well are Feed the Future -supported research activities designed to address major global challenges and spur agricultural development across initiative Focus Countries?
10. How well has the initiative leveraged private sector participation to support agricultural and nutritional outcomes?
11. How well is Feed the Future promoting policy reform at the national and regional level, including implementation of policy reform?
12. How well have Feed the Future MEL approaches achieved accountability for commitments Feed the Future has made? Has the Feed the Future MEL system supported improved programming and how?

c. Overview of Evaluation Design

The overall design for this performance evaluation of the Feed the Future Global Initiative is a mixed methods design that will incorporate both quantitative and qualitative methods for data collection and analysis to address each question. Starting with an analysis of the evaluation questions and an extensive document review, the team worked with the Internal Evaluation Panel (IEP) to identify which questions would be answered across all 19 focus countries, aligned countries, USAID/Bureau for Food Security (BFS) programs, and the five field work countries.

A synopsis of the diverse data sources, data collection and analysis methods that we will use to answer each evaluation question and its sub-questions is found in Annex A (Evaluation Design Matrix.) In most cases, evaluation questions will be answered with a combination of FTFMS data analysis, data mining from selected documents, and drilling down further with key informant interviews. Online surveys of different sets of stakeholders will allow us to gather multiple views within a short period of time, and follow-up interviews may be conducted as themes emerge. By combining performance data from the FTFMS and any pre-existing survey data, with online surveys of large numbers of stakeholders, key informant interviews with decision-makers and implementers of the Feed the Future initiative, we will be able to triangulate the information that is collected. The five country visits will provide an opportunity for the collection of richer data, contextualizing the quantitative performance results, and explaining how the initiative is implemented at the country level.

The following sections provide details on data collection methods and sources that will be used, both quantitative and qualitative, and on the methods that will be used to analyze data from each source.

The primary source of quantitative data that will be used for this evaluation is performance monitoring data extracted from the Feed the Future Monitoring System (FTFMS) database. In addition, we will draw on quantitative data from FTF population based surveys (PBS), activity baseline survey reports, beneficiary surveys, and Country Demographic and Health Survey (DHS) Reports.

FTFMS Data

The Feed the Future Monitoring System (FTFMS) is a web-based whole of government database developed to collect and house data for Feed the Future performance monitoring indicators. Data collection for FTF indicators began in 2011. The Feed the Future indicators were designed to measure progress toward achievement of each result at each level of the Results Framework (goal, first level objectives, IRs, and Sub-IRs). Achievement of results is based on meeting annual and life of project (LOP) targets. Based on the selection of these indicators and availability of sufficient data points, one should be able to examine progress to date in meeting annual and LOP targets at the output level to assess the likelihood of meeting targets at the sub-IR level, and from those data, assess the likelihood of achieving results at the IR level and so on up through each level of the results framework. During the later years of program implementation, there should be sufficient data to test the causal linkages that comprise the Feed the Future theory of change.

FTF Indicators

FTF uses four categories of performance monitoring data as follows:

1. Required (R) indicators are high-level impact indicators used to measure the goal and the first-level objectives in the FTF Results Framework (RF).

2. Required if Applicable (RiA) indicators are outcome level indicators used to measure the second-level objectives in the FTF RF, which are the eight Intermediate Results. They must be incorporated if country programming supports these results.

3. Whole of Government (WOG) indicators are RiA indicators on which all U.S. Government Agencies with programs aligned with FTF and the Global Agriculture and Food Security Program will report.

4. Standard (S) indicators are optional indicators that represent "best practices" in tracking project and activity-level progress in areas of key interest to the FTF strategy.

There are a total of 53 FTF indicators, and of these, eight are required and 21 are required if applicable as described above. Of these 21, there are 13 outcome level indicators to measure the second-level objectives, or IRs, and eight project level output and outcome WOG indicators, or sub-IRs. Table 1 lists the required indicators that measure the FTF Goal and the first-level objectives and the required if applicable indicators used to measure the eight IRs.

Table 1: Required Indicators and Required if Applicable Indicators for Feed the Future Goal, First-Level Objectives and Intermediate Results.

Indicator	Measures
Required Indicators	
Prevalence of poverty	Goal: Sustainably Reduce Global Poverty and Hunger
Prevalence of underweight and stunted children	
Prevalence of Poverty: Percent of people living on less than $1.25/day	First Level Objective: Inclusive Agriculture Sector Growth
Percent change in agriculture GDP	
Per capita expenditure (as a proxy for income) of USG targeted beneficiaries	
Women's Empowerment in Agriculture Index (WEAI)	
Prevalence of stunted children under five years of age	First Level Objective: Improved Nutritional Status
Prevalence of wasted children under five years of age	
Prevalence of underweight women	
Prevalence of underweight children under five years of age	
Required if Applicable Indicators – IR Level	
Gross margin per hectare, animal or cage of selected product	IR 1 Improved Agricultural Productivity
Value of incremental sales (collected at farm level) attributed to FTF implementation	IR 2 Expanded Markets and Trade
Percent change in value of intra-regional trade	
Number of firms (excluding farms) or Civil Society Organizations (CSOs) engaged in agricultural and food security-related manufacturing and services now operating more profitably (at or above cost) because of USG assistance	IR 3 Increased Investment in Agriculture and Nutrition-Related Activities
Value of new private sector investment in the agriculture sector or food chain leveraged by FTF implementation	

Indicator	Measures
Number of jobs attributed to FTF implementation	IR 4 Increased employment opportunities in targeted value chains
Prevalence of households with moderate to severe hunger	IR 5 Increased Resilience of Vulnerable Communities and Households
Depth of Poverty: Mean percent shortfall relative to the $1.25 poverty line	
Prevalence of children 6-23 months receiving a minimum acceptable diet	IR 6 Improved Access to Diverse and Quality Foods
Total quantity of targeted nutrient-rich value chain commodities produced by direct beneficiaries that is set aside for home consumption	
Prevalence of exclusive breastfeeding of children under six months of age	IR 7 Improved Nutrition-Related Behaviors
Prevalence of anemia among women of reproductive age	IR 8 Improved Use of Maternal and Child Health Services

We will use the FTFMS database to assess performance to date based on data reported for all relevant Feed the Future indicators. Analysis for country specific (or regional) programs will assess performance compared to annual and LOP targets related to each level of the Feed the Future RF. We will draw on this analysis for specific indicators depending on the focus of each evaluation question. For example, data analysis from the eight outcome level indicators, both required and required if applicable, will be used to answer Evaluation Question 2: "How has the Feed the Future initiative performed against each of its eight intermediate results outlined in the Feed the Future RF across focus countries?" Data analysis from all Feed the Future FTF indicators at each of the four levels of the framework will be used to answer the second part of Evaluation Question 2: "Does the progress made across the eight intermediate results to date, coupled with changes in impact-level indicators, provide evidence that Feed the Future is on track to achieve its five-year goals of reducing poverty and stunting by 20%?"

Population Based Survey (PBS) Data

PBS data are collected in Zones of Influence (ZOI) selected by each focus country. The ZOI represent specific areas within a country where Feed the Future resources and interventions will be focused. Each focus country is responsible for impact level results only within the ZOI they have selected. Baseline data are collected once a ZOI is established. Interim surveys are currently being carried out, and if available in time, this evaluation will incorporate data collected to measure progress toward meeting targets for Feed the Future impact level indicators, to measure goals related to poverty and nutrition, and to assess progress toward meeting targets for Feed the Future outcome-level indicators at the IR level. Table 2 lists those required (R), required if applicable (RIA) and standard (S) indicators collected through population-based surveys in the ZOI.

Table 2: Zone of Influence Population-based Survey Indicators

Prevalence of anemia among women (RIA)	Prevalence of households with hunger (RIA)
Prevalence of stunted children (R)	Prevalence of exclusive breastfeeding (RIA)
Prevalence of wasted children (R)	Prevalence of Poverty (R)
Prevalence of underweight women (R)	Depth of Poverty (RIA)
Prevalence of anemia among children (S)	Daily per capita expenditure (RIA)
Prevalence of underweight children (R)	Women's Empowerment in Agriculture Index (R)
Prevalence of children receiving MAD (RIA)	Prevalence of women consuming nutrient-rich value chain commodities (S)
Women's Dietary Diversity (S)	Prevalence of children consuming nutrient-rich value chain commodities (S)

Online Survey Data

Quantitative data from online surveys will be used in several different ways depending on the evaluation question. The primary uses of the data will be to augment or compare findings from reviews of selected key resource documents; to obtain initiative wide data on specific topics; and to compare findings from the perspectives of focus country programs, regional country programs, and aligned country programs. Separate online surveys will be designed for: 1) Focus Countries; 2) Aligned Countries; and 3) Regional Country Programs. The survey data collection instruments will be pre-coded to correspond to specific evaluation questions prior to transmittal. The majority of questions will be based on multiple choice options or Likert scales that examine, for example, the degree of: use and usefulness of Feed the Future research products, accessibility of research and learning products and lessons learned, and usefulness and clarity of guidance from FTF/SPPM/MEL M&E Guidance Series. The following stakeholders will be targeted in each of the three programming subsets:

Focus countries: 1) the USAID Feed the Future Team Lead; and 3) the Feed the Future M&E Manager.
Regional programs: 1) the USAID Feed the Future Team Lead for the regional mission; and 2) the Regional Feed the Future M&E Manager.

Aligned programs: 1) the Mission coordinator for the FTF portfolio; and 2) the Mission M&E Manager

II) Qualitative data

Key Informant Interview (KII) and Focus Group Discussion (FGD) Data

Qualitative data will be collected through phone interviews with selected stakeholders in Washington, DC, and other areas of the country. In-person KIIs and FGDs will be conducted in each of the five focus countries selected for field work. Interviewees and group participants will be selected based on a determination of those stakeholders that are best suited and able to provide responses that will address specific evaluation questions. For many of the questions, a range of stakeholders will be selected to provide multiple points of view and to help eliminate bias through triangulation. We include a Key Informant Interview Matrix that incorporates an illustrative list of individuals (referred to by titles or roles) that will be interviewed in Annex B in this report. It provides a list of key stakeholders that will be interviewed through KIIs for each of the evaluation questions along with the types of information we want to obtain from each interview. It also includes individuals to select for participation in focus group discussions. The contents from this matrix will be used to develop data collection instruments for key informant interviews and focus group discussions.

Online Survey Data

In addition to the qualitative data described above, online surveys will also collect qualitative data. In addition to the multiple choice and Likert scale questions, the survey will include targeted open-ended questions to elicit more nuanced information that is best captured in narrative form. This data will be coded to identify categories and themes.

Primary data collection

Primary data collection includes key informant interviews, focus group discussions, direct observation, and online surveys as described above.

Secondary data collection

Secondary data collection comprises accessing key documents provided by BFS, various data sets and reports from the FTFMS, and identifying and downloading documents available online from the Feed the Future website and related websites (e.g., Agrilinks, FEEDBACK). Secondary data sources range from the Feed the Future Results Framework, Feed the Future M&E Guidance Documents, Multi-Year Strategy (MYS) documents, Feed the Future Annual Portfolio Reviews, Progress Reports and 2012/2013 Scorecards; Feed the Future policy guide, policy matrices, and related reporting; Country Investment Plans (CIPs); impact evaluation (IE) and performance evaluation reports; Annual Activity Reports from the Focus Countries selected for fieldwork and country program specific RFs; products produced through the BFS Research Agenda and the Feed the Future Learning Agenda; and program funding information. The Evaluation Question Matrix specifies which documents, website data, and so forth will be used to address each evaluation question, and the type of data that will be used from each of those sources.

Sampling Strategy

The evaluation team used non-probability, purposive sampling for the selection of country programs, based on specific criteria, to select the five Focus Countries These criteria are presented below.

Criteria for Selection of Focus Countries for Field Work

The team began its selection process by drawing from the BFS-proposed list of nine countries. The criteria BFS used to develop this list included size of program, to get a range of different sizes in the sample; proximity to a regional mission; good data quality and availability; presence of other USG programs (e.g., FFP, USDAA, FFProgress, McGovern-Dole, etc.); absence of major security issues; the baseline size of the agriculture program; and inclusion of a variety of programs that cover the Feed the Future Results Framework. The second step in the selection process was to cross-reference the list of nine countries with the four countries included in the Dexis proposal, which used some of the same criteria plus criteria based on ZOI population and poverty and stunting rates. We augmented these criteria using input from senior technical advisors on the evaluation team, based on their knowledge of Feed the Future programs gained from field experience in the list of nine countries. For example, the team used this additional input to select Ghana because it is a New Alliance Country, and the program includes resilience programs and investments from FFP, FFProgress and McGovern-Dole programs. Uganda was selected because in addition to the criteria used by BFS and Dexis, development has occurred along with decades of humanitarian crises and Feed the Future responses. Guatemala was selected over Honduras because Feed the Future investments have been more diverse.

Based on these combined criteria and additional considerations, the following countries were recommended for fieldwork.

Table 3: Country Field Visits

Country	Program Size	Variety of Programs Highlights	Regional Mission Proximity	Data Quality/ Availability	Other USG Programs	ZOI Population Size	Poverty Rate	Stunting Rate
Ghana	Large	good example of local solutions; comprehensive program built on existing agriculture work under GFSR	co-located with regional program		New Alliance program MCC Compact Country	5.2 million	22.2%	36.1%
Uganda	Large/ Mid-size	market systems facilitation approach, resilience programming		strong data and evidence available through various surveys and evaluations		13.7 million	32.8%	32.99%
Malawi	Mid-size	built on former agriculture programming			presence of FFP, FFPr, and McG-D, integration with FFP	4.9 million	66.7%	49.2%
Guatemala	Mid-size	diverse program with strong results	close to regional mission	good data quality and availability	presence of FFP, FFPr, and McG-D	1.5 million	5.9%	67.4%
Bangladesh	Large	diverse program with strong results	easy access to regional mission	good data quality and availability	presence of FFP, FFPr,McG-D	27.4 million	40.5%	37.1%

Criteria for Selection of Aligned Countries

Purposive sampling techniques were also used to select Aligned Countries for inclusion in the scope of this evaluation. The primary criterion used to select Aligned Countries was a cumulative funding threshold of $25 million of USAID Feed the Future agriculture funding over the timeframe from 2011 to 2015. Therefore, the countries selected include any country that received $25 million or more during the five-year time period ranging from 2011 to 2015. The rationale behind this criterion is that a $25 million threshold equates to an average of $5 million or more per year over the time period in which we can expect to see results. As such, countries that only received funding in FY 2015, all of which are lower than $25 million, would not be included, given that they have not had funding for a long enough time period to reasonably expect results and/or to begin programming activities. In addition, this criterion captures countries that have had long-standing (within the 2011 – 2015 timeframe) moderate aligned investments, as well as countries that have received funding more recently, but at higher levels.

Through this selection criterion, the team has identified the following five Aligned Countries to be included in the scope of this evaluation: Burma, Democratic Republic of the Congo, Egypt, Nigeria, and South Sudan.

e. Methodology for Quantitative and Qualitative Data Analysis

Coding Strategy

All data collection instruments will be pre-coded before application to support the data analysis phase of the evaluation. Specifically, the evaluation team will use a systematic and standard coding approach across all the qualitative datasets. The three qualitative datasets will include the document review, KII data, and FGD data.

For the document review data, the team will develop a pre-coded data collection tool that maps to each of the evaluation questions. In addition, the data collection tool will include provisions for identifying themes and trends across the data as it is being collected. These themes and trends will then be linked to codes which will inform the coding strategy developed for the other qualitative datasets.

For both the survey and KIIs, phone interview and FGDs datasets, the team will develop an initial coding strategy based on the evaluation questions. This coding system will be used to pre-code the data collection instruments to allow for easily identifiable subcategories of information within the survey data and interview transcripts that map against the relevant evaluation questions. In addition, the team will develop a more detailed code-book for each dataset that identifies themes based on the Feed the Future theoretical framework associated with the specific evaluation questions being addressed, as well as the document review that will be used to code the qualitative data once it has been collected. All transcripts from interviews and text will be uploaded into NVivo, the qualitative data analysis software. While the code-books will provide a standard format for coding all of the text within that particular dataset, they will remain flexible to allow for the addition of newly identified trends during the analysis phase.

For an initial set of transcripts and survey text, two of the members will double-code the set of transcripts/text to cross-check for coding alignment across the set. Once a common understanding and practice for aligned coding has been established, each transcript will be coded by a single team member to ensure timeliness given time and cost constraints. However, the team will conduct periodic checks of the other team member's coding strategy to ensure alignment across all transcripts.

The quantitative datasets will be coded to map to the relevant set of evaluation questions that the dataset will be used to address. This coding will be done for organizational purposes, given that subsets of the larger quantitative datasets will be used to address multiple evaluation questions. This will ensure accessibility as well as accountability of the various quantitative datasets being used for analysis.

Qualitative: KIIs and FGDs

Responses from KIIs, phone interviews and FGDs will be recorded and uploaded into our evaluation database at the end of each day. However, there will be occasions in which key informants or participants in focus group discussions do not want to be recorded. In these cases, the team member assigned to taking notes during the interviews will prepare a transcript of the interviews or discussions at the end of the day from each of the pre-coded questions. The team member leading the interview or discussion will review the completed transcription to confirm or possibly add additional responses not caught by the note taker. Completed transcripts will be prepared at the end of each day for subsequent input into the database.

At the home office, evaluation team members assigned to the analysis of qualitative data will begin the process of identifying initial categories of information based on responses to questions and, once completed, assign codes for those categories. The next process will be to identify themes within each of those categories. Once the range of themes has been identified per category, additional coding will be applied. We will use intra-rater reliability mechanisms based on multiple coders to increase the reliability and justification of the codes before analysis begins.

Thematic analysis will be used to produce findings for each question. For some questions, findings will be compared across key informants to capture the range of experience and views between, for example, USG in-country representatives and Mission Feed the Future Managers and Mission Food for Peace Officers, between members of donor coordination community representatives, and Feed the Future in-country representatives (including USAID), and between Mission AORs/CORs and Feed the Future Program Managers, Food for Peace Officers and Implementing Partners.

Quantitative

The team will use basic quantitative manipulation methods to run summary statistics of indicator data extracted from FTFMS. This will include developing summary data of indicators by categories such as geographic specifications, sex disaggregation, etc., as well as trend analysis over time, from 2011-2015, and progress against baseline and target values. Using these summary statistics, the team will examine relevant data and indicators for each applicable evaluation question. For example, the team will look at indicators such as "number of farmers and others who have applied improved technologies or management practices over time with USG assistance." Then there will be analysis of the trend over time, whether increasing or decreasing; cross-tabulating with other indicators within and across intermediate results to form a more comprehensive understanding of Feed the Future programming impact, and mapping the results to the results of Sub-IR 1.1., IR 1, the objective level, and goal level to determine causal pathway analysis. The team will triangulate this quantitative data with other quantitative and qualitative data as necessary to provide a comprehensive analysis and evidence based findings that will feed into recommendations.

Database and Software

The Evaluation team will utilize two of the highest quality industry-standard software tools for the majority of data analysis, NVivo and STATA. For the qualitative data analysis, the team will use NVivo to store, code, and analyze the qualitative data collected from the KIIs and FGDs as well as the surveys. To the extent possible, the KIIs and FGDs will be audio-recorded to ensure completeness and accuracy of data. All data collection instruments will include specific language on informed consent. For those individuals who do not wish to have the interviews audio-recorded, notes will be taken by two of the team members *and cross-referenced, to ensure completeness of data capture.* These notes will be electronically captured to ensure compatibility and ease of compilation with the transcripts for analysis. All the qualitative data, including the verbatim transcripts, typed notes from the KIIs and FGDs, and exported survey data from SurveyMonkey, will be uploaded into NVivo for qualitative data analysis. Both the electronically recorded verbatim transcripts as well as the typed-notes of the KIIs and FGDs will be compiled into one master dataset and coded using the same coding strategy. Demographic information for all interview data will be provided, but any identifying information will be removed to maintain anonymity. In addition, the team will use Excel for the document review data collection and analysis process.

For the quantitative analysis, the team will use Excel and statistical software STATA to store, organize, and analyze all quantitative data. All relevant indicator data on FTFMS will be exported from FTFMS and imported into STATA to conduct statistical analysis. In addition, depending on the type of quantitative data extracted from the document review and the surveys, the team will use STATA and/or Excel based on the level and type of analysis required. STATA will be used to conduct statistical analysis including summary statistics of the FTFMS dataset, identifying trends and trajectories of specified sets of data, and examining correlations between various indicators. Excel will be used to collect and store all quantitative data, regardless of that particular dataset being used in STATA for statistical analysis.

f. Limitations of the Evaluation

Limitations of this evaluation are based on the following issues:

1. **Lack of sufficient number of data points in FTFMS**. Our initial examination of this crucial database indicates that there is a lack of data for certain RiA FTF indicators used to measure achievement of results at the Intermediate Result level to develop performance trends across the Initiative. Data for many of those indicators rely on population-based surveys conducted in focus country ZOI. This relates to the second limitation.

2. **Availability of PBS data.** Interim data collection for PBS is currently underway in many focus countries. These data sets may not be available to the team in time to answer questions on progress in reaching goal level indicators on poverty and malnutrition (Evaluation Question 2).

3. **Limitations on use of data obtained from fieldwork.** Given that the five countries selected for fieldwork were based on a range of criteria (purposive sample) rather than through a random selection process, the findings from the analysis of data derived from the fieldwork will not be representative of the total population of focus countries. The findings from these data sets can only be used as an additional source of data for triangulation purposes, except in certain circumstances depending on the evaluation question.

3. Management Plan

a. Team Members and Roles and Responsibilities

The Dexis home office will provide a qualitative evaluation methods specialist and one mid-level evaluation specialist to provide support for the five in-depth country studies and interviews with BFS-managed programs and regional programs. A Senior Agricultural Research Advisor, Derek Byerlee, will supplement the team. A local consultant will be hired in each country to support logistics, arrange meetings with implementing partners and other stakeholders, and provide any potential translation services.

Table 4: Roles and Responsibilities of Key Personnel

Team Member	Roles and Responsibilities
Lee Briggs, *Evaluation Team Leader*	Primarily responsible for team management, coordinating and synthesizing inputs from all team members. Responsible for development and implementation oversight of the evaluation work plan, including timely production and completion of all deliverables and reporting products. Contributes to development of evaluation design, evaluation workplan, data collection instruments, data analysis plan, report writing and presentations to IEC, EOC. Responsible for quality assurance of all evaluation activities and outputs. Conducts field work in three of the countries selected for in-depth assessment. Substantially responsible for client engagement in the field and for client relations.
Dr. Patricia Vondal, *Senior Evaluation Specialist*	Develops, in consultation with Team Leader, the evaluation design, evaluation workplan, and data collection instruments. Supervises, in consultation with the team leader, data analysis. Contributes content to final evaluation report, under the direction of the Team Leader.
Allyson Bear and William Fiebig: *Senior. Technical Advisors*	Based on their areas of expertise related to the FTF program, provide inputs into the evaluation design, review data collection instruments and provide recommendations for improvement, conduct KIIs and FGDs in Washington, DC, and in countries selected for field work, providing analysis of same. Provide technical comments and recommendations on draft evaluation report.
Laurie Chamberlain, *Senior. Communication Specialist*	Professional editing and writing of evaluation report

b. Home Office Program Management Unit Oversight and Logistics

Operational oversight and logistical support. The Dexis PMU ensures that activities and deliverables are regularly tracked, that the timeline is appropriately met, and that the evaluation team receives all administrative and logistical support necessary. Ioannis Sophocleous, the Project Associate, is the primary liaison with the Team Lead and the evaluation team and is responsible for day-to-day administrative and logistical support and contractual compliance. The Dexis PMU arranges for the availability of all resources needed to complete the evaluation, including travel and transportation, meeting arrangements, equipment and field accommodations, and report preparations.

Technical oversight. Natasha Hsi, Director of Monitoring, Evaluation, and Learning, provides technical and management oversight to ensure that all products and processes are of the highest technical quality. The Dexis PMU has instituted weekly check-in meetings with the team and the IEP. The PMU will look at the consistency, coverage, and quality of all data gathering procedures and provide feedback accordingly to the evaluation team on any potential data collection or quality issues.

Communications. The Team Lead is the primary point of contact with the IEP and EOC. The evaluations methods specialists (Senior Evaluation Specialist and one mid-level evaluation specialist), the Senior Technical Advisors, and Senior Agricultural Research Advisor report to the Team Lead. The Team Lead reports to the Dexis PMU which communicates primarily with the BFS COR, Dr. Emily Hogue. **Table 5** delineates the role of Dexis PMU and the evaluation team members for each key activity and deliverable.

Table 5: Evaluation activities and roles of the evaluation team and the Dexis PMU.

Activity	Role of Evaluation Team	Role of Dexis PMU
Evaluation team planning meeting	Review scope of work, process for developing the workplan, and communication procedures.	Lead meeting, onboard all evaluation team members, arrange logistics of evaluation team meeting, arrange and coordinate first meeting of IEP and EOC.
Workplan	Develop detailed timeline, team responsibilities, data analysis plan and writing responsibilities.	Review workplan.
Evaluation design	Develop and finalize data collection and analysis methods, evaluation protocol and data collection instruments.	Review evaluation design. Contact key informants for scheduling of interviews. Contact in-country points of contact for FTF to arrange country visits.

Activity	Role of Evaluation Team	Role of Dexis PMU
In-brief meetings (country visits)	Teams of two people (comprised of combinations of the team lead, senior evaluation specialist, senior technical advisors and the mid-level evaluation specialist) will travel to 5 countries.	Maintain regular check-ins with travel teams, ensure smooth logistics, follow-up on security issues related to countries and brief team accordingly.
Regular weekly updates and reports	Team Lead or delegate participates in phone calls. Team lead produces weekly and monthly reports	Review weekly and monthly reports Maintain weekly updates with IEP and monthly updates with EOC.
Debriefings with the IEP, EOC, Missions, FTF teams	Evaluation team to debrief with IEP and EOC at the conclusion of the in-depth country visits.	Arranges debriefing with IEP and EOC. Processes expense reports from field visits.
Draft evaluation report	Draft evaluation report	Quality review of draft report.
Final report	Review and incorporate IEP and EOC comments.	Consolidate comments from the IEP and EOC. Quality review of final deliverable. Formatting and copy editing of final report.
Final presentation	Develop PowerPoint presentation	Quality review and formatting of presentation
Posting of final report	Approves final report.	Obtain all final approvals from the IEP, EOC and BFS. Posting to the DEC and any required DDL files.

c. Data Quality Control

Methods that will be employed to ensure quality control of data collection

The Evaluation team will ensure data quality and validity throughout the evaluation process, during both the data collection and analysis phases. During the data collection phase, for the qualitative data from KIIs and FGDs, the team will ensure data completeness and accuracy through producing verbatim transcripts from audio-recordings, as well as having two people taking notes at each interview where individuals do not wish to be audio-recorded. In addition, the team will enforce data standards across multiple data collection teams by using standard data collection tools and formats, and ensuring standard understanding of coding practice across all the different data collection instruments. All interview transcripts will include relevant demographic data.

During the data collection phase, the team will include interview questions regarding data collection and reporting concerns that should be flagged pertaining to the FTFMS datasets.

During the data analysis phase, the team will conduct a rapid assessment of the compiled datasets to identify missing data, understand sources of error and bias, and reconcile data from different sources in order to allow for comparison of completeness and accuracy of data. For the quantitative data, the team will ensure data quality and validity by running multiple checks such as ensuring that data lines up in the appropriate columns, sorting fields of data and checking for discrepancies, performing statistical summaries and comparing before and after data transformations, and examining outliers through statistical models and graphs to identify potential sources of data contamination. Through these multiple types and levels of data quality and validity checks, the team will maintain transparency on data limitations.

d. Data Management and Security

Dexis has described how it will transmit collected data into formal databases or software platforms for data analysis under the section describing databases and software platforms that will be used for this evaluation. To ensure that respo
ndent information is kept secure and confidential, the databases and software platforms will be password protected. Evaluation team members that are responsible for cleaning data, downloading interview data, and using data sets for analysis will each be provided with a unique password. Transcripts will include titles/positions of persons interviewed through KIIs, phone interviews, and FGDs, but not names. To ensure confidentiality, Dexis will scrub any names of individuals that may have been included inadvertently in the transcript.

e. Ethical Considerations

Under the Code of Federal Regulations, Title 45, this evaluation would fall under exemptions 3 and 5 of the IRB exemption list. Dexis will follow the Office of Human Research Protections guidance on informed consent for key informant interviews and focus group discussions both in the United States and in the five countries selected for country visits. Dexis will conform to 46.116 general requirements for informed consent for all key informant interviews and focus group representatives.

4. Evaluation Design Attachments

a. Evaluation Question Matrix

Evaluation Questions	Units of Analysis	Data Sources	Data Collection Methods	Data Analysis Methods
	19 Focus Aligned Regional Fieldwork BFS			

Questions 1-6: Assess the Feed the Future initiative's progress against its strategic goals and objectives in the field of operation

Question 1: Adherence to and progress across the Feed the Future RF across the initiative. How well have the (a) strategies and (b) implementation of programs followed the RF and the causal pathways identified therein? Parts a. and b. of this question are treated separately below.

Evaluation Questions	Units of Analysis	Data Sources	Data Collection Methods	Data Analysis Methods
1. a. How well have **strategies** followed the RF and causal pathways?	19 Focus countries Regional programs Aligned countries	FTF Results Framework FTF Guide FTF Guidance on integrating Climate Smart Agriculture into strategies Evaluation Synthesis of FTF Learning Agenda Evaluations ***From each focus and aligned country and regional program*** Multi-Year Strategy document PMP and RF Policy Matrices	Data mining from documents listed No additional data collection.	*This question is addressed through structured reviews and analysis of key documentation using FTF guidance as the reference point. Assessment of how well implementation of programs followed the FTF RF and causal pathways is supplemented with data from KIIs conducted in five focus countries selected for field work and evaluation reports.* Qualitative – Structured Document Reviews **Step 1:** Create an analytical tool based on FTF strategy guidance documents to assess of adherence to FTF RF and causal pathways based on relationships of IRs to Objectives and Goals. Use PMPs and Results Frameworks from focus, regional and aligned country programs to compare against FTF RF for this analysis. **Step 2:** Conduct a structured document review from MYS documents per focus and aligned country and per regional program to provide additional information for assessing adherence to the FTF RF and causal pathways. Combine with findings from Step 1 to provide an overall finding per country program

Evaluation Questions	Units of Analysis	Data Sources	Data Collection Methods	Data Analysis Methods
	19 Focus Aligned Regional Fieldwork BFS			**Step 3**: Conduct a comparative analysis of findings on adherence to the RF and causal pathways across: a) focus countries; b) aligned countries; and c) regional programs.
1. b. How well has **implementation** of programs followed the RF and causal pathways	19 Focus countries Regional programs Aligned countries 5 Fieldwork countries	Same documents as above plus: FTF Annual Portfolio Reviews Official strategy change memos Additional documents for countries selected for field work include annual reports from each FTF activity and evaluation reports KII data from interviews in DC and in field	Data mining of documents listed to the left KIIs in focus countries selected for field work with: Mission FTF coordinator/manager Mission FTF AORs Mission FTF M&E Manager Mission Program Officer and M&E Manager Mission Gender Advisor, Nutrition Advisor	Qualitative – Structured Document Reviews **Step 1**: Extend the analytical tool created to address Evaluation Question 1.a to assess fidelity to the RF and causal pathways in the implementation of the FTF program through a review of FTF Annual Portfolio Reviews and Strategy Change Memos for each focus country, regional program, and aligned country, review FTF annual portfolio reviews and any official strategy change memos for evidence with respect to degree of fidelity to the FTF RF and causal pathways for each year of program implementation. For focus countries selected for fieldwork, include in this document review the Mission FTF Portfolio Review documentation and data from identified evaluation reports (as relevant to this analysis). Develop findings from analysis per focus, regional and aligned country programs. **Step 2**: Compare findings from Step 1 (above) with the findings from Evaluation Question 1a (above). Is there consistency between findings on strategy per program and findings on implementation on an annual basis? Develop findings based on this analysis to add to the findings from Step 1 to answer this question. **Step 3**: Conduct a comparative analysis of findings on adherence to the RF and causal pathways across: a) focus countries; b) aligned countries; and c) regional programs.

Evaluation Questions	Units of Analysis	Data Sources	Data Collection Methods	Data Analysis Methods
	19 Focus Aligned Regional Fieldwork BFS		FGDs with each IP to include COP, senior technical staff and the IP M&E Manager	**Additional Analysis for Responding to this Question based on selected field work countries:** Qualitative – Structured Document Review **Step 4** Identification of relevant evaluation reports and structured content review for analysis related to FTF strategy implementation that can be used to provide further information related to findings from Step 3 for countries selected for field work. Qualitative - KII and FGD Data Analysis **Step 5.**Conduct a content analysis from KIIs and FGDs conducted in fieldwork countries on implementation of FTF RF and Mission Strategy, and any reasons for divergence from FTF RF and strategy based on causal pathways. Prepare Overall Findings from Field **Step 6:**Compare results of content analysis from KIIs conducted in field work countries with findings from assessments and evaluation documents of those programs that pertain to the Mission FTF strategy and strategy implementation in relationship to FTF RF to extend those findings from document analysis (for those specific field countries) from Step 3. Do findings from the analysis of these data sources converge (per fieldwork country)? Do these findings provide explanation to understand divergence from strategies?

Question 2: How has the Feed the Future initiative performed against its 8 IRs across focus countries? Does the progress made against the 8 IRs to date, coupled with changes in impact level indicators, provide evidence that Feed the Future is on track to achieve its five year goals of reducing poverty and stunting by 20%?

Evaluation Questions	Units of Analysis 19 Focus Aligned Regional Fieldwork BFS	Data Sources	Data Collection Methods	Data Analysis Methods
2. a. How has the FTF initiative performed against each of its 8 IRs outlined in the RF across focus countries?	19 Focus countries	FTFMS data	no additional data collection	*This question will be addressed through a quantitative analysis of data from the FTFMS database for each focus country. As available, these data will be augmented from IEs and interim updates from baseline survey data.* Quantitative – FTFMS Data **Step 1**: For each Focus Country, conduct statistical analysis comparing actual performance values to date to targets set each year, for each indicator used to measure each of the 8 IRs. The analysis will aggregate data across all activities contributing to a given indicator. **Step 2**: To the extent we have sufficient data points, prepare performance trend lines for each focus country per IR based on analysis completed under Step 1. Include the LOP target per indicator.
2. b Does the progress made against the 8 IRs to date, coupled with changes in impact-level indicators, provide evidence that FTF is on track to achieve its 5 year goals of reducing poverty and stunting by 20%? **PLEASE NOTE: Analysis to answer this question can only be done for**	19 Focus countries	FTFMS data FTF Results Framework from each focus country FTF Policy Matrix Reports PBS baseline and interim data as available.	no additional data collection	Augment the analysis conducted under 2a carrying out the following steps: Quantitative: FTFMS data, and as available, updated baseline information and data from IEs. **Step 1:** Conduct statistical analysis per focus country comparing actual performance values to date to targets set each year to measure national level impact goal level indicators on prevalence of poverty and prevalence of underweight children, and for national impact indicators for measuring Inclusive Agriculture Sector Growth and for Improved Nutritional Status especially of Women and Children.

< table>

Evaluation Questions	Units of Analysis	Data Sources	Data Collection Methods	Data Analysis Methods
focus countries where interim data from PBS are available.	19 Focus Aligned Regional Fieldwork BFS			**Step 2**: Prepare performance trend line for each focus country based on the analysis conducted under Step 1 for each of the national impact indicators. Include the LOP targets. **Step 3**: Examine the FTF Results Framework for each of focus countries to document the sub-IRs and indicators each focus country has selected to support progress at the IR level. **Step 4**: Using the FTFMS data, repeat analytical procedures conducted under Step 1 for each sub-IR included in each focus country's FTF Results Framework that is associated with one or more of the eight IRs. Repeat procedures for each indicator used by the focus country to measure the sub-IRs. **Step 5**: Prepare a performance trend line for each focus country based on the analysis conducted under Step 4 for the sub-IRs per Mission including LOP targets per indicators. **Step 6**: Conduct an analysis comparing the trajectory of performance to date against targets for each IR, and the trajectory of performance to date against targets of each sub-IR supporting the each of those IRs and make a determination of the likelihood of achieving targets at the IR level based on this analysis. **Step 7**: Using the results of the analysis from Step 6, compare with the results of the performance trends calculated for each national impact level indicator (separate analysis for portions of FTF result framework associated with inclusive agricultural growth and poverty reduction and for portions of FTF results framework associated with improved nutritional status and

Evaluation Questions	Units of Analysis	Data Sources	Data Collection Methods	Data Analysis Methods
	19 Focus Aligned Regional Fieldwork BFS			reduction in stunting) to determine whether five year goals for poverty reduction and for stunting by 20% is achievable.

Question 3: The implementation and effectiveness of the selectivity and focus approach within given country or regional portfolios. See 3 a - c below:

3.a. (i) How have value chain approaches been applied and (ii) what have been the successes and challenges to focusing resources on strategic and limited value chains?

Evaluation Questions	Units of Analysis	Data Sources	Data Collection Methods	Data Analysis Methods
3 a i How have value chain approaches been applied?	19 Focus countries 5 Fieldwork countries	FTF Guide FTF Q&A FTF Policy Guide **Per Country:** Multi Year Strategy FTF Annual Portfolio Reviews FTF Annual Reports per country **Additional Resources to be consulted in field countries.** Host government annual plans and reports related to implementation of CIPs, CAADP plan, and MCC Compact Investment Portfolio Mission PAD Mission FTF portfolio description	Phone interviews for Washington, DC and other stakeholders in the US. Include BFS/ARP, BFS/CSI, Office for FFP FTF program managers and advisors associated with value chain work, FFP Officer FTF whole of government active agencies on VC (USDA, Trade) FTF non whole of government partners on VC	*For the purposes of this question, strategic is defined as value chains selected on the basis of country agricultural/economic assessments, overlap with other programs in the ZOI, and be complimentary to the country MYS. Limited is defined on FTF guidance that value chains should be limited to 3 -4 within the ZOI/s. We will address this question by examining MYS documents and Annual FTF reports from Focus countries that describe whole of government contributions to selected value chains, dollar values invested in resources per annum. Additional document reviews will be done in the five focus countries selected for field work to provide additional detail. KIIs will provide data on the issue of how well FTF has focused resources on those value chains, and how strategic the value chain selection is.* Qualitative – Structured Document Review **Step 1**: This assessment will be based on reviews of: MYS, FTF Annual Portfolio Reviews, CIPs, CAADP (focus countries in Africa), and MCC Compacts (if an MCC country). Create an analytical tool to assess how strategic the value chains selected for the FTF program are based on criteria including: alignment to CIP, country agricultural strategies, and CADDP plans (for focus countries in Africa), complementarities with interventions

Evaluation Questions	Units of Analysis	Data Sources	Data Collection Methods	Data Analysis Methods
	19 Focus Aligned Regional Fieldwork BFS	Activity Annual Reports per contributing project	Initiative contacts (GAFSP) A sample of KII from universities (MSU, Cornell) FGDs with IPs: implementing activities that include value chains on approaches applied. Include IP COP, DCOP, M&E Specialist, VC Program Officers and technical staff	from other donors, multi-lateral institutions related to the value chain and its success. Analysis findings will be prepared according to the following categories: 1: not strategic at all, 2. Partly strategic: alignment with country owned plans **or** complements with interventions by other organizations, institutions, bilateral donors. 3. Strategic: value chain is in alignment with country owned plans and interventions by other organizations, institutions, bilateral donors. **Step 2:** Prepare findings per focus country. **Assessments from five focus countries selected for field work** Qualitative: Structured Document Review **Step 3:** Prior to fieldwork, review country specific documents listed to the left for details of inputs and activities related to each value chain. Review annual reports and documentation of annual portfolio reviews to determine success to date based on an assessment of performance to date on value chain related indicators, explanations of performance to date. Qualitative: KII and FGD Data **Step 4:** Conduct content analysis of KIIs and FGDs for views on how strategic is the selection of value chains, rationale for selection and performance to date based on analysis of relevant FTFMS data conducted under Step 3. Prepare separate findings from Mission, from IPs, government, other USG actors, private sector partners.

Evaluation Questions	Units of Analysis	Data Sources	Data Collection Methods	Data Analysis Methods
	19 Focus Aligned Regional Fieldwork BFS			**Step 6:** Are KII findings from each group consistent? Do KII findings confirm findings from analysis of financial budget and expenditures per year, and FTFMS performance data? <u>Summary Analysis</u> **Step 7:** Prepare findings to address evaluation question based on analysis of data collected from the five focus countries; Include insights based on the perspectives from the specific country context.
3. a.ii What have been the successes and challenges to focusing resources on strategic and limited value chains?	19 Focus countries 5 Fieldwork countries VC	same documents as noted above FTFMS Data Reviews FTF Annual Portfolio Reviews Performance and Impact Evaluation Reports FTFMS data KII data	Data mining of documents listed Analyze of results report data Analysis of evaluations Phone interviews with selected stakeholders in Washington, DC KIIs in focus countries selected for field work: (list by bullet)	*We will address the issue of success to these approaches through the analysis of performance data from relevant FTFMS indicators associated with value chain activities and use of findings from available IEs, and performance evaluations. Those findings will be supplemented by a review of FTF Annual Portfolio reviews for data and descriptions of success and challenges. Those findings will be supplemented through KIIs conducted in the five countries selected for field work, and reviews of country specific documents. FTF Annual Portfolio reviews* Quantitative: FTFMS data **Step 1:** Draw on Analysis of FTFMS data sets conducted under Evaluation Question 2 for indicators related to success of value chains per focus country. Prepare summaries on how well targets are being met for each focus country. Findings will provide measures of success. Qualitative: Structured Document Review **Step 2:** Using Annual Reports, BFS portfolio reports, document relevant data that describes and provide evidence of success to

Evaluation Questions	Units of Analysis	Data Sources	Data Collection Methods	Data Analysis Methods
	19 Focus Aligned Regional Fieldwork BFS		Additional in-country KIIs where relevant: MOA market and planning staff. Local and regional trade reps (EGAC, RATIN, COMESA) USAID Trade Hubs CILSS Club du Sahel Farmer/producer groups Key VC actors	approaches taken disaggregated by the typology of VC approaches prepared under Step 1 conducted for the first part of this question. At the same time, identify and document relevant data that describes challenges to these approaches and what the focus country missions are doing to address these challenges (to address the third part of this question (see below) **Step 3**: Augment results of analysis from step 1 and step 2 with findings from relevant evaluation reports that can be associated with specific value chain approaches. Document findings on outcomes from implementation of value chain approaches, findings related to successful and unsuccessful outcomes, and challenges. **Step 4**: In focus countries selected for field work augment document review to review with annual reports submitted by IPs implementing activities that incorporate value chain work to gain deeper understanding of success factors, unsuccessful outcomes to date (targets aren't being met) and challenges of approaches applied in each country. Qualitative: KII/FGD data **Step 5**: Conduct content analysis of KII data for information about how implementation of the value chain approaches are creating success, explanation of factors that underpin success challenges Summary Analysis: **Step 6**: Overall analysis. Do findings from document reviews of different data sources and from analysis of KII data support the

Evaluation Questions	Units of Analysis	Data Sources	Data Collection Methods	Data Analysis Methods
	19 Focus Aligned Regional Fieldwork BFS			successes, and lack of success to date from different approaches as analyzed from FTSMS data, If not, reexamine data sources. **Step 7:** Summarize findings on successes and challenges across focus countries, disaggregated by type of VC approaches implemented.

Question 3b. How well has the initiative focused implementation and concentrated resources in appropriate (in terms of size and agro-ecology) geographic zones?

Evaluation Questions	Units of Analysis	Data Sources	Data Collection Methods	Data Analysis Methods
3. b. How well has the initiative focused implementation and concentrated resources in appropriate (in terms of size and agro-ecology) geographic zones?	19 Focus countries 5 Fieldwork countries	Strategic and program documents per country: MYS FTF Portfolio Reviews Baseline data reports from ZOI per country Strategy Change Memos as they pertain to ZOI Documentation from CSI FTFMS Mission FTF PMP/M&E Plans FTF Evaluation Reports at the activity/country level Budget/ Financial data Data from KIIs	Data mining from documents **KIIs in US:** **BFS/CSI, Office of FFP** **KIIs in Field-work Countries:** Mission FTF Coordinator/ Manager FTF A/CORs Mission FTF M&E Manager FFP Officer IP staff (COP, DCOP, M&E)	Qualitative- Structured Document Review **Step 1:** through review of strategic and program docs, develop matrix of intention of implementation scope and reach per country - by zones (i.e. which zones are targeted and the populations aimed to be reached: either as direct beneficiaries - market actors and producers and indirect beneficiaries such as consumers). **Step 2:** Per country - develop matrix of resources allocated and implemented within zones - financial/activities (number, type), etc. per year. **Step 3:** Compare allocation and implementation of resources within zones with plans and determine whether to date the actual allocation of resources and implementation of activities is in line with planned focusing of resources and activities per country. **Step 4:** Review Annual reports, FTF and BFS portfolio reviews per mission and findings from appropriate evaluation reports to identify information/explanations that support result of

Evaluation Questions	Units of Analysis	Data Sources	Data Collection Methods	Data Analysis Methods
	19 Focus Aligned Regional Fieldwork BFS		Local government partners within Ministry of Agriculture and Commerce and/or Food Security network.	previous step, or if not, document for further assessment of document information. Qualitative: KII data **Step 5**: Conduct content analysis of KII data from DC for findings on issues related to resource allocation and implementation within zones, reasons why actions taken if deviation from intentions as originally planned and compare with results of document reviews and analysis. Do they support results of analysis from previous steps (steps 3 and 4). **Step 6**: Conduct content analysis of KII data from countries selected for field work for explanations related to concentration of resources in zones as planned, resource allocation and implementation. Do they support findings from analysis of other data sets? Where do they diverge? Document and re-review data sets.
Question 3c. Are the proportions of households being reached in the ZOI sufficient to plausibly achieve the targeted impacts?				
3. c. Are the proportions of households being reached in the ZOI sufficient to plausibly achieve the targeted impacts?	19 Focus countries 5 Fieldwork countries	FTFMS data KIIs data BFS/CSI reports As available, IE reports, and updated baseline data on households within zones	Data mining from documents **KII in US with:** BFS/CSI and Office of FFP **KIIs with:** Country reps from other USG partners with relevant activities	Quantitative Analysis **Step 1**: For each focus country, use FTFMS data from indicators providing data on #s of households reached at the zone level to determine proportions of households being reached in the ZOI, per year. **Step 2**: Conduct a trend analysis to determine % change (increase) in proportions of households being reached each year versus annual and LOP targets in each zone. **Step 3**: Compare findings with analysis of FTF RF impact level targets (at the ZOI level) conducted under Evaluation Question

Evaluation Questions	Units of Analysis	Data Sources	Data Collection Methods	Data Analysis Methods
	19 Focus Aligned Regional Fieldwork BFS	**Additional documents for focus countries selected for field work** evaluation reports Mission Portfolio Reviews of FTF program Annual Reports for Mission activities pertaining to ZOI CIPs and Annual Reports based on CIPS CAADP plans and annual reports on implementation (for field work countries in Agriculture)	Mission FTF Coordinator/Mgr. FTF A/CORs Mission FTF M&E **Mission FFP Officer** Group Interviews with key staff from each IP appropriate to this question Online Survey Data from Focus Countries	# 2 to determine the rate of change necessary to achieve those targets, and whether the % change (increase) in the proportions of households being reached from step 2 is less than, equal to, or greater than that – a result of equal to or greater than indicating "sufficient to achieve targeted impacts". **Step 4:** Analyze data from online survey responses from focus countries on proportion of households being reached to obtain a finding across all focus countries and per focus country. Determine whether those findings support analytical findings from Step 3. Document Reviews **Step 5** Conduct structured document review for documents collected for each of the five field work countries to broaden understanding of totality of activities implemented from all partners involved in agriculture and nutrition interventions within each zone and results to date that could support achievement of targets. Qualitative Analysis **Step 6** Conduct content analysis of the KIIs for opinions on likelihood of achieving targeted impacts and to identify factors supporting/hindering plausibility of achieving targeted impacts based on results of quantitative analysis. Summary Analysis of Findings Across Data Sources **Step 7** Determine the extent to which findings from steps 4 and 5 support findings from analysis of quantitative data. Document findings that explain lack of convergence, alternative views of

Evaluation Questions	Units of Analysis	Data Sources	Data Collection Methods	Data Analysis Methods
	19 Focus Aligned Regional Fieldwork BFS			plausibility, and factors that support or hinder achievement of targets.

Question 4: How and to what extent have Feed the Future interventions, both Mission- and centrally- managed, helped build human and institutional capacities for the agricultural and nutrition/health sectors? (Mission and centrally managed HICD programs are treated separately in 4.a and 4.b. below)

Evaluation Questions	Units of Analysis	Data Sources	Data Collection Methods	Data Analysis Methods
4.a How and to what extent have **Centrally managed** Feed the Future interventions helped build human and institutional capacities for: i) the agricultural sector? ii) the nutrition/health sector?	Operating Unit of Analysis: BFS Global Health Bureau Scope: FTF focus countries (aligned and focus) where centrally managed awards report quantitative data related to capacity building (institutional and/or human). If	FTFMS (standard and custom indicators) FTF Guide FTF Indicator Handbook FTF Guidance Series on HICD BFS annual portfolio reviews on HICD Documents from HICD Mechanisms (MEAS, LEAP, innovate) and M&E plans Documents from FTF Food Security Innovation Center – Research program in HICD Annual reports and evaluations from centrally funded activities with HICD activities (list to be provided by USAID)	Data mining: within documents listed in "data sources" and additional documents found. On-line survey of focus countries, aligned countries, regional country programs that are recipients of centrally managed HICD interventions on how well aligned with their own HICD strategy, and degree to which those have contributed to their FTF portfolio	Quantitative **Step 1:** Identify indicators from the FTF M&E framework that reflect human and institutional capacity development (HICD). **Step 2:** Identify custom indicators on HICD from USAID/W centrally managed programs. Also review data reported through GH/PPR for nutrition/health sector. **Step 3:** Conduct analysis (from all BFS HICD awards reporting on identified indicators) to look for trends in human/institutional capacity for interventions and performance against targets for each year. Stratify by agricultural and nutrition activities. Stratify by category of person/institutional if possible as well (e.g. ministry official vs. farmer, Ministry of Agriculture vs. Private Company). **Step 4:** Prepare summaries on how well targets are being met 1) in top 5 awards, and 2) across BFS awards. **Step 5:** Analyze on-line survey data responses stratified by focus, aligned, and regional country programs, and within by agriculture and nutrition sector for degree of contribution from centrally managed HICD interventions and how well those were aligned with their HICD strategy. **Step 6:** Develop findings on level of integration with their own HICD strategy and degree of contribution across: 1) focus

Evaluation Questions	Units of Analysis	Data Sources	Data Collection Methods	Data Analysis Methods
	Units of Analysis 19 Focus Aligned Regional Fieldwork BFS centrally managed activities do not report quantitative standard or custom indicators for HICD, assume no HICD activities.		outcomes in both sectors Conduct phone interviews with BFS C/AORs, and/or Implementing Partners of a sub-set of 5 centrally-managed programs, based in the U.S. that contribute HICD indicators in FTFMS.	countries, 2) aligned countries, and 3) regional country programs. Qualitative: Structured document review **Step 7:** Develop a listing of top 50% (dollar value) of Washington-based awards with human and institutional capacity building activities included in their mandate, disaggregated by ag/nutrition and with dollar values. Document HICD activities, dollar value, anticipated results articulated in the award documentation in a matrix. Include listing in evaluation report as a reference of the universe of work happening at this level. Select top 5 awards in terms of dollar value for in-depth analysis. **Step 8:** For 5 selected awards, review documents cited in Data Source column. Document relevant data that describes and provides evidence of success to approaches taken for HICD. Identify and document relevant data that describes challenges to these approaches and what BFS is doing to address these challenges. **Step 9:** Compare findings of quantitative analysis with findings of document review. Do findings converge? **Step 10:** Select FDGs with stakeholders of top 5 awards based on the listing. Qualitative: KII phone interview and FGD data **Step 11:** Conduct content analysis of KII and FGD data on individual and institutional capacities for a. the agricultural sector? b. nutrition/health sector

Evaluation Questions	Units of Analysis	Data Sources	Data Collection Methods	Data Analysis Methods
	19 Focus Aligned Regional Fieldwork BFS			Compare with findings of document review and quantitative analysis. <u>Summary Analysis</u> **Step 12:**Develop findings based on comparison of analytical findings from each data source, record themes, in response to Q 4.1a and Q4.1b.
4.b How and to what extent have *Mission-managed* Feed the Future interventions helped build human and institutional capacities for: i) the agricultural sector? ii) nutrition/health sector?	Regional Aligned 19 Focus countries 5 Fieldwork countries	FTFMS data Custom indicators obtained through reports and M&E plans FTF Guide FTF Indicator Handbook FTF Guidance Series on HICD FTF MYS FTF Annual portfolio reviews (5 field work countries) From 5 selected focus countries: PMPs for Mission FTF portfolio and M&E Plans from selected implementing partners	<u>Data mining:</u> within documents listed in "data sources" and additional documents found. Conduct KIIs and/or FDGs in 5 field visit countries: with Program Office, FTF Team Leads, C/AORs, and Implementing Partners of top 2-3 awards (dollar value) in field visit countries. Subjects: methods for assessing progress in HICD, targeting methods	The scope will we use to address this question is as follows: FTF countries (regional, aligned and focus) where awards report quantitative data related to capacity building (institutional and/or human). If awards do not report quantitative standard or custom indicators for HICD, assume no HICD activities. In-depth qualitative work will be limited to 5 focus countries, and 2 regional missions. <u>Quantitative: FTFMS Data</u> **Step 1:** Identify indicators from the FTF M&E framework that reflect HICD. **Step 2:** Identify custom indicators on HICD from Mission managed programs in 19 focus and aligned countries, as well as regional missions (data call). **Step 3:** Identify indicators on nutrition (3.9.1 funds) HICD that are reported through global health channels but are applicable to FTF (data call). **Step 4:**Analyze data (from all BFS HICD awards reporting on identified indicators) to look for trends in human/institutional capacity for interventions and performance against targets for each year., Stratify by agricultural and nutrition activities, and

Evaluation Questions	Units of Analysis	Data Sources	Data Collection Methods	Data Analysis Methods
	19 Focus Aligned Regional Fieldwork BFS	whose activities include human/institutional capacity development Program descriptions, annual reports and evaluations of top 2-3 projects (dollar value) with HICD components in the 5 field work countries, 2 aligned countries, 1 regional mission. FDGs (field work countries) On-line Survey (aligned countries, regional mission)	and progress against targets, strengths and limitations of HICD activities, sustainability of efforts related to ongoing contribution to FTF / Food Security programs, contribution of HICD interventions to outcomes related to agricultural and nutritional interventions. KIIs with host country government officials and other recipients of HICD to validate	within, by category of person/institutional as well (e.g. ministry official, farmers, Ministry of Agriculture, farmer cooperatives, health clinics, health workers, private company, regional institutions (e.g., ECOWAS). **Step 5:** Prepare summary of findings on how well targets are being met 1) the subset of countries identified for in-depth review, and 2) across all FTF focus countries, aligned countries, and regional Missions reporting. <u>Qualitative: structured document review</u> **Step 6:** Develop a listing of activities with human and institutional capacity building activities included in their mandate, disaggregated by ag/nutrition and with dollar values. Include listing in evaluation report as a reference of the universe of work happening at this level. Select countries for in-depth review (5 field visit, 2 aligned, 2 regional Mission). **Step 7:** For operating units selected for in-depth review, review documents cited in Data Source column. Document relevant data that describes and provides evidence of success to approaches taken for HICD. Identify and document relevant data that describes challenges to these approaches and what operating units are doing to address these challenges. **Step 8:** Compare findings of quantitative analysis with findings of document review. Do findings converge? **Step 9:** Conduct quantitative analysis of on-line survey data stratified by focus, aligned and regional country programs and within by agricultural interventions and nutritional interventions

Evaluation Questions	Units of Analysis	Data Sources	Data Collection Methods	Data Analysis Methods
	19 Focus Aligned Regional Fieldwork BFS		qualitative and quantitative data collected. On-line survey focus countries, regional missions, and aligned countries on utility of guidance for HICD, HICD indicators for reporting on results of HICD interventions and opinion on the sustainability of HICD interventions	on degree of contribution of HICD interventions to outcomes, likelihood of sustainability of interventions in terms of ongoing contributions to country food security programs, and utility of BFS HICD guidance and indicators to measure and to promote outcomes. Qualitative: KII and FGD Data **Step 10:** Conduct content analysis of Mission and IP KII data and FGDs for findings on progress against targets, contribution of HICD interventions to agricultural and nutrition outcomes, sustainability of HICD contributions to ongoing implementation of FTF and country food security programs, **Step 11:** Conduct content analysis of KII data with recipients of HICD training on quality and utility of interventions, opinions on HICD contribution to FTF and country food security goals, and likelihood of sustainability in terms of ongoing contribution to those program and goals. **Step 12:** Compare findings from Step 1 and Step 2 to determine the degree of convergence between Mission/IP and recipients of HICD interventions, note discrepancies between sets of findings. Final Analysis **Step 13:** Compare findings from each data set to determine the degree of convergence with findings from analysis of FTFMS HICD indicator data and HICD custom indicator data. Note discrepancies, try to resolve by re-examining appropriate data sets. Note those discrepancies that cannot be resolved.

Evaluation Questions	Units of Analysis	Data Sources	Data Collection Methods	Data Analysis Methods
	19 Focus Aligned Regional Fieldwork BFS			**Step 14:** Prepare analytical findings in response to Q 4.2a and Q4.2b using quantitative and qualitative findings.

Question 5. How and to what extent have Feed the Future interventions promoted gender-inclusive agricultural sector growth and improved nutritional status of women through equitable and strategic integration of women and men in agriculture and nutrition programs?

Evaluation Questions	Units of Analysis	Data Sources	Data Collection Methods	Data Analysis Methods
5. a. How and to what extent have Feed the Future interventions promoted gender-inclusive agricultural sector growth and improved nutritional status of women through equitable and strategic integration of women and men in agriculture and nutrition programs?	19Focus countries Aligned countries 5 Fieldwork countries	FTFMS data FTF Guide FTF Indicator Handbook FTF Gender Guideline MYS as available, updates to baseline from mid-term data collection (relevant indicators) from ZOI Report: What Do We Know About the Feed the Future Initiative's Progress toward Nutrition Goals? Results of a Global Landscape Analysis	Data mining: within documents listed in "data sources". **Phone Interviews with USAID stakeholders** USAID/W: FTF Gender Advisors, BFS/CSI, MEL staff, Office of FFP **KIIs and FGDs in the field:** Mission FTF M&E Manager, Gender Advisors, FTF Team Leads for Agriculture and Nutrition, C/AORs, Program Officer,	*Our primary means of addressing this question will be through quantitative analysis of relevant data sets to examine progress in promoting gender-inclusive agricultural sector growth and improved nutritional status of women through equitable and strategic integration of women and men in agriculture and nutrition programs. Reviews of MYS documents will be conducted to examine the application of FTF Gender guidelines into gender strategy and planned interventions per focus, aligned and regional country programs. A more in-depth treatment of this question for focus countries selected for field work will be conducted using additional country specific documents and KIIs.* <u>Quantitative: FTFMS and related data sets</u> **Step 1:** Identify indicators that capture gender inclusivity in agricultural interventions under FTF based on FTF Gender Guidelines, especially as it pertains to the three key gender objectives listed in the gender guidance. **Step 2:** Identify FTFMS indicators related to integration of women and men in agriculture and nutrition activities from the FTFMS. Some of these will be gender specific and some will be indicators that are disaggregated by gender. Disaggregate by agriculture and nutrition programs.

Evaluation Questions	Units of Analysis	Data Sources	Data Collection Methods	Data Analysis Methods
	19 Focus Aligned Regional Fieldwork BFS	reports from MEL Learning Agenda research on gender integration Synthesis of Evaluations on the FTF Learning Agenda **Additional** *Data Sources from focus countries selected for field work* Mission and FTF Project Gender Assessments Mission Food Security PADs (Gender Analysis) Relevant evaluations Annual Reports KII and FGD data	M&E Specialist, FFP Officer FGD with each Implementing Partner	**Step 3:** Draw on analysis of FTFMS indicators on gender and gender disaggregation conducted under Evaluation Question 2. Conduct an analysis of the data sets to look for trends in women's participation against targets per year and LOP targets. Disaggregated by focus, aligned and regional country programs and by agriculture and nutrition indicators. To the extent possible, stratify by category of person (farmer, agricultural processor, etc.) **Step 4:** Draw on analysis of data from FTFMS indicators on nutritional status of women and analysis determining likelihood of goal achievement related to nutrition status conducted under Evaluation Question 2. Disaggregate by focus, aligned and regional country programs. **Step 5:** For the Focus countries that have applied the Women's Empowerment in Agriculture Index, incorporate into the analysis data sets from the Women's Empowerment in Agriculture baseline report and updates to this data set. Incorporate findings from report: What Do We Know About the Feed the Future Initiative's Progress toward Nutrition Goals? Results of a Global Landscape Analysis **Step 6:** Prepare summaries on how well targets are being met in 1) countries targeted for in-depth review and 2) across FTF portfolio disaggregated by focus, aligned and regional country programs. Qualitative: Content Analysis of Key Documents

Evaluation Questions	Units of Analysis	Data Sources	Data Collection Methods	Data Analysis Methods
	19 Focus Aligned Regional Fieldwork BFS			**Step 7**: Compare strategies related to gender in MYS documents to gender guidelines to assess application to the strategy.. **Step 8:** Extend document analysis for countries selected for fieldwork to determine extent to which the country MYS gender strategy, Mission and FTF Gender Assessments and the Mission Food Security PADS are reflected in IP Annual Reports and Country Level FTF Annual Reports. Qualitative: KII data and phone interview data **Step 9:** Conduct a content analysis of KII and FGD data to determine views and opinions on how well FTF as a whole is developing and implementing strategies and activities to promote equitable and strategic involvement of women and men in agriculture and nutrition activities. Compare findings between different persons and groups interviewed in Washington and in the field. Do findings converge? What accounts for different points of views? Final Analysis **Step 11**: Do the findings from the analysis of each data set converge? Document findings at variance, try to resolve by a review of analysis from data sets. Present overall findings related to the evaluation question, disaggregate by focus, aligned and regional country programs. What are the challenges? What are the successes?

Evaluation Questions	Units of Analysis	Data Sources	Data Collection Methods	Data Analysis Methods
Question 6. a) How have Feed the Future interventions integrated nutrition into value chain activities? If so, how? b) Do results differ if nutrition objectives are an integral part of the value chain work? (a and b are treated separately)				
6. a. How well have Feed the Future interventions integrated nutrition into value chain activities?	19 Focus countries Aligned Regional Fieldwork BFS 5 Fieldwork countries 19 Focus countries Aligned countries	FTF Guide MYS FTF Annual portfolio reviews Relevant VC program descriptions and evaluations (Mission level) Previous evaluations of VC work initiative-wide Mission Food Security PADs	Data mining from documents. Online survey KIIs with BFS/CSI, Office of FFP	<u>Qualitative: Structured document review and case selection</u> **Step 1:** Draw on results from Question 3 on typology of VC approaches. **Step 2:** Determine criteria for classification of activities into: no integration, minimal to moderate integration, significant integration. **Step 3:** Classify all activities into 1 of 3 categories. **Step 4:** Select 6 examples to conduct deeper analysis (2 in each category). Amount and thoroughness of documentation around the intervention and outcome/impact level data should be considered when selecting the cases. <u>Qualitative: KII and FGD data</u> **Step 5:** Content analysis of KII data and develop findings. <u>Quantitative Analysis: On-line survey data</u> **Step 6:** Analyze data from online survey from questions on integration of nutrition into value chain activities, difference it has made for those countries where nutrition was integrated **Step 7:** Compare findings from analysis of on-line survey data, and findings from document reviews from Step 3 to determine how well nutrition interventions have been integrated into value chain activities. Document findings that diverge from overall findings and reexamine data analysis from all sources to try to resolve. Summarize findings, themes, commonalities, and differences across 6 cases. Identify and document findings that

Evaluation Questions	Units of Analysis	Data Sources	Data Collection Methods	Data Analysis Methods
	19 Focus Aligned Regional Fieldwork BFS			cannot be resolved for future analysis. Prepare analytical findings for questions.
6. b. Do results differ if nutrition objectives are an integral part of the value chain work? If so, how?	19 Focus countries	FTFMS FTF Indicator Handbook KII/FGD data	KIIs/FGDs in countries selected for field work with Mission FTF Team Leads, Nutrition Specialists, FFP Officer and IPs,	Quantitative: FTFMS Data **Step 1:** Identify select nutrition indicators from the FTF M&E framework that could plausibly be linked to VC interventions and draw on analytical results from statistical analysis conducted under Evaluation Question 2 based on performance vs. targets on those indicators. **Step 2:** Using the categorization defined in 6.a analyze data to see if there is a difference in nutrition outcome data by level of nutrition integration compared to countries that have not integrated nutrition objectives in value chain activities. Qualitative: KII/FGD data **Step 3:** Conduct content analysis of KIIs and FGDs on integration of nutrition objectives into value chain work. What difference has it made for nutrition outcomes in those value chains where nutrition interventions were integrated? Summary Analysis **Step 4:** Do findings from KII/FGD analysis provide any support or further clarity on findings from Step 2?

Evaluation Questions 7-12: Using the Feed the Future Guide as a reference point, assess the performance and management of the Feed the Future Initiative as a whole, specifically in terms of relevance, effectiveness, and sustainability.

Question 7: The effectiveness of Feed the Future's focus on country ownership. How well has Feed the Future fostered country ownership of the Feed the Future program in Focus Countries to support sustainability of outcomes?

Evaluation Questions	Units of Analysis	Data Sources	Data Collection Methods	Data Analysis Methods
Per Focus Country program				
7. a. How well has FTF fostered country	19 Focus countries		data mining from documents listed	Our approach to answer this question is primarily based on interviews with a range of relevant FTF stakeholders in

Evaluation Questions	Units of Analysis	Data Sources	Data Collection Methods	Data Analysis Methods
ownership of the FTF program in Focus Countries to support sustainability of outcomes?	19 Focus Aligned Regional Fieldwork BFS 5 Fieldwork countries	MYS CIP KII and FGD data **Additional documents from field include** Annual Mission Portfolio Reviews of FTF program Host government annual reports related to implementation of CIPs, Annual FTF Reports evaluation reports as relevant covering government participation	KIIs with FTF managers and stakeholders in Washington KIIs and FGDs in countries selected for field work with FTF Country Coordinator, Mission FTF staff, Mission Director, and USG reps in country KIIs with host country partner reps involved in CIP development and implementation	*Washington, and in the countries selected for field work, with the FTF Country Coordinator, Mission FTF staff, Mission Director, and USG in-country representatives associated with FTF. Data will be compared from various perspectives along with documentation on what Focus Countries are doing to foster ownership. Results of analysis of KII data will be compared to government views. Document reviews of MYS and CIPs per focus country will be used to examine government role in their FTF program. Additional documentation will be consulted in the field to try to gain additional information on the government role, and the extent to which they lead efforts.* <u>Qualitative – Structured Document Review</u> **Step 1:** Review contents of MYS documents per focus country to CIP documents to determine respective roles and areas of planned collaboration. Are they in alignment with respect to government role? The results of this review are mainly to inform the evaluation team's understanding of the collaboration between the USG and Government in planning and implementation for the country FTF program. **Step 2:** Review the additional documents listed under data sources for the countries that will be included in the field work. Is there any evidence of actions that supports government ownership of the FTF Program in addition to human and institutional capacity development interventions? <u>Qualitative Analysis: KIIs and FGDs</u>

Evaluation Questions	Units of Analysis 19 Focus Aligned Regional Fieldwork BFS	Data Sources	Data Collection Methods	Data Analysis Methods
				Step 3: Conduct content analysis of KIIs conducted in Washington for views on how well country ownership is being fostered to ensure sustainability of outcomes, how this is being promoted, and what could be done by Focus Country USG participants to improve the extent to which governments do have ownership. **Step 4**: Conduct content analysis of KIIs and FGDs from each country selected for fieldwork. Compare views between different government actors participating in FTF and among different USG FTF participants. Prepare findings based on range of views. Document range of findings from each set of FTF stakeholders interviewed. Where is there a convergence? What at are the areas of disagreement? Document what USG participants in country are doing to foster ownership to sustain outcomes, comments on how this can be improved. Document comments from government on what they think is necessary to assume ownership? Should be done to take greater ownership of the program. **Step 5**: Compare findings from Steps 2, 3 and 4 and prepare overall findings. Include summary of key actions taken to promote country ownership and key recommendations for improvement.

Question 8.cWhat has been the Feed the Future's contribution to influencing and leveraging multi-lateral institutions and initiatives?

Evaluation Questions	Units of Analysis	Data Sources	Data Collection Methods	Data Analysis Methods
8. What has been the FTF's contribution to influencing and leveraging multi-lateral institutions and initiatives, specifically: i) G8 and the New Alliance ii) CAADP iii) Global Agriculture and Food Security Program (GAFSP) iv. Consultative Group for Agricultural Research	19 Focus Aligned Regional Fieldwork BFS 19 Focus countries BFS centrally managed programs Regional programs	MYS FTF Annual Reports Investment Portfolios from focus countries annual reports from multi-lateral institutions and initiatives BFS/ARP/Policy Division Portfolio Reviews BFS/MCI Portfolio Reviews on finance, risk and investment themes and markets and trade theme Agrilinks website Learning documents from Strategy on policy research/policy guidance MEL products BFS/Research Division Annual Portfolio Reviews research contributions to GAFSP from research documents/reports research funded by BFS/Research Division	Data mining from documents Phone interviews with: BFS managers from ARP and MPI initiatives FTF Deputy Coordinator for Diplomacy at Dept. of State representatives of USG partners that contribute to each multi-lateral institution and initiative representatives of the various multi-lateral institutions and initiatives for views on FTF contributions KIIs in field: Country FTF Coordinator and	**Step 1:** Identify whole of government partners associated each with multi-lateral institutions and initiatives listed in Evaluation Question 8. Qualitative - Structured Review of Documents **Step 2:** Review documents listed to identify FTF programs frameworks, guidance documents that represent FTF contribution to multi-lateral institutions and initiatives and for evidence of leadership role taken by FTF (either USAID or other USG partners). **Step 3:** Construct a matrix of intellectual contributions to each multi-lateral institution and initiative. Qualitative - KII and phone interview data **Step 4:** Conduct a content analysis of KIIs conducted in Washington with BFS ARP and MPI managers, FTF Deputy Coordinator for Development, and USG partners to obtain further data on FTF contribution to influencing and leveraging. **Step 5:** Conduct a content analysis of KIIS with USG partners for views/details on FTF contributions. **Step 6:** Conduct a content analysis of KIIs with representatives of multi-lateral institutions and initiatives for views on FTF contributions and use of intellectual products identified in Step 5. **Step 7:** Conduct a content analysis of KIIs conducted in field for information on how these contributions are affecting FTF program in country, views on value of that contribution. Summary Analysis: Combining findings from each Step

Evaluation Questions	Units of Analysis	Data Sources	Data Collection Methods	Data Analysis Methods
	19 Focus Aligned Regional Fieldwork BFS	New Alliance Cooperation Frameworks and reports	Mission FTF Program Manager Country representatives from multi-lateral institutions and initiatives	**Step 8:** Combine findings from each group of KIIs to develop an overall finding on FTF contribution to augment findings from Step 3 to answer the Evaluation Question and to provide evidence of contribution to the evolving food security landscape.

Question 9. The effectiveness, relevance and collaboration in Feed the Future's implementation of its research strategy. How well are FTF supported research activities designed to address major global challenges and spur agricultural development across initiative Focus Countries

Evaluation Questions	Units of Analysis	Data Sources	Data Collection Methods	Data Analysis Methods
9. How well are FTF - supported research activities designed to: i) address major global challenges; and, ii) spur agricultural development across initiative Focus Countries?	19 Focus countries, 5 Fieldwork countries	FTF Guide, MYS, FTF Research Strategy, BFS/Research Division Annual Portfolio Reviews, Annual Reports - as they relate to research, Portfolio Reviews - as they relate to research, ARP Program Documents, FSIC Program Area Factsheets, Evaluation Reports of Research Activities, KII data, Online survey data	Document review, Online survey of Focus Countries, Phone interviews with stakeholders in DC with: BFS/FTF Research Lead/s (or equivalent), Private sector company partner representatives, USG Partners (Dept. of Agriculture's Norman Borlaugh Science and Technology	Quantitative: Analysis of online survey data **Step 1:** Analyze responses to questions on significance, utility of research products, and application of research findings. Qualitative: Analysis of comments from online survey **Step 2:** Conduct content analysis of comments on research activities/products from online survey. Qualitative: Structured Document Reviews **Step 3:** Through document review, determine: i) what is included as "global challenges" and; ii) what is included as research to promote agricultural development. **Step 4:** Conduct content analysis of documents reviewed to identify the types of research questions being addressed and categorize by "global challenge" it/they address. **Step 5:** Conduct content analysis of documents reviewed to if/how research activities are spurring agricultural development across the initiative countries by focusing on the research activity designs – objectives/goals

Evaluation Questions	Units of Analysis	Data Sources	Data Collection Methods	Data Analysis Methods
	19 Focus Aligned Regional Fieldwork BFS		Fellowship) representatives Partners in US/and Field work countries (to be extracted from "ARP Programming by Country" documents: University partners representatives International Institution partners (CGIAR, International Rice Research Institution) representatives Private sector company partner representatives USG Partners (Dept. of Agriculture's Norman Borlaugh Science and Technology	**Step 6:** Conduct content analysis of research outputs/follow-ons to determine if /how research findings were followed up on (i.e. mentioned in follow-on programs - affecting program design, etc.) (for i and ii). <u>Qualitative: Analysis of KII data</u> **Step 7** Conduct content analysis of KII and phone interview data on research significance to global challenges and application in field settings, document reasoning behind commissioning particular research and post-research activities. <u>Summary Analysis</u> **Step 7:** Compare findings from analysis of on-line survey data (Steps 1 and 2) with findings from Steps 6 and 7 to determine if there is any convergence on significance and applicability of findings from research pursued related to global challenges that affect agricultural development. Document outlier findings that show the range of opinions and outcomes from application of research findings in field settings.

Evaluation Questions	Units of Analysis	Data Sources	Data Collection Methods	Data Analysis Methods
	19 Focus Aligned Regional Fieldwork BFS		Fellowship) representatives KIIs in Field-work Countries: Mission FTF Team Lead, FTF M&E Specialist	

Question 10: How well has the initiative leveraged private sector participation to support agricultural and nutritional outcomes? Note: Treated a) on global level and b) on country level

Evaluation Questions	Units of Analysis	Data Sources	Data Collection Methods	Data Analysis Methods
How well has the initiative leveraged private sector participation to support agricultural and nutritional outcomes? GLOBAL LEVEL	BFS/MPI 5 Fieldwork countries Global and Regional programs	FTF RF FTF Guide FTFMS FTF Indicator Handbook BFS/ MPI annual portfolio reviews New Alliance reports PPP documents (to be provided by BFS/MPI) MPI activity description documents, reports, evaluations, budgets and annual expenditures for programs on a global and regional level that leverage	Phone interviews with: BFS staff in Partnership, Marketing and Innovation Office Reps from USG Agencies with a role in private sector partnerships (e.g. Treasury, Commerce, OPIC, Office of US Trade Representative) FTF liasons in US and multinational corporations	Qualitative: Structured Document Review Step 1: Review documents cited in Data Source column specific to MPI programs/activities to identify TF role at the global and regional level disaggregated by programs under the 4 themes and corresponding budgets, and within those 4 themes, disaggregated by programs to support agricultural and to support nutritional outcomes. Step 2: Map out the results of Step 1 against FTF Results Framework to determine alignment with agricultural and nutritional outcomes (e.g., Sub-IRs relevant to IR 1, 2, 3 and 6) in support of first level objectives and the FTF goal. Step 3: Review Annual BFS/MPI portfolio reviews information on results to date by thematic area, including data on leveraging private sector investment, increasing private sector engagement and benefits related to agricultural and nutritional outcomes mapped against the FTF RF (from Step 2).

Evaluation Questions	Units of Analysis	Data Sources	Data Collection Methods	Data Analysis Methods
	19 Focus Aligned Regional Fieldwork BFS	and increase private sector engagement based on MPI's 4 themes: 1) finance, risk and investment, 2) PPPs, 3) commercialization of technologies and innovations, and 4) markets and trade. e.g., New Alliance for Food Security and Nutrition, FTF Grow Africa platform, FTF Private Sector Program, FTF Partnering for Innovations, FTF Assets and Market Access Innovation Lab, Agriculture Fast Track, etc. Data from KIIs	participating in FFP in focus countries KIIs in countries selected for field work with Country FTF Coordinator, USG country reps associated with private sector activities, Mission FTF Portfolio Coordinator and private sector representatives associated with global and regional programs on effectiveness of global/regional programs on leveraging private sector investments and increasing private sector involvement in	**Step 4:** Review evaluations, assessments of programs for additional data that would support findings from Step 3 on support to agricultural and nutritional outcomes in focus, aligned and regional country programs. Quantitative - FTFMS and On-line Survey Data **Step 5:** Identify Private Sector indicators from the FTF M&E framework that reflect funding at a global level. Use results from analysis of performance against targets conducted under Evaluation Question 2 to augment findings from document review. **Step 6:** Analyze aggregated data on dollars of private sector investment leveraged by global and regional FTF programs on an annual basis to look for trends in private sector investments. **Step 7:** Analyze responses from on-line survey data on contribution of global and regional activities on their country (or regional) programs and how well they are integrated with country specific programs/activities to increase private sector participation and to leverage private sector dollars to support agricultural and regional outcomes? Summary Analysis **Step 8:** Conduct a meta-analysis of findings from key steps above to respond to evaluation question. Qualitative: Phone interview data from Washington stakeholders and KII data from the field **Step 9:** Conduct content analysis of KII and phone interview data. a) Compare results with findings from document reviews

Evaluation Questions	Units of Analysis	Data Sources	Data Collection Methods	Data Analysis Methods
	19 Focus Aligned Regional Fieldwork BFS		support of country-specific agricultural and nutritional outcomes. On-line survey data on contribution of global, regional activities on in-country programs, how well coordinated/aligned with any country specific activities to promote private sector participation.	and quantitative analysis of FTFMS data and data on dollar amounts of private sector investment leveraged by FTF global and regional programs related to outcomes in the agricultural and nutritional sector based on alignment with FTF RF. b) Do analytical findings from KII data from the five field countries support findings on contribution of global and regional programs to specific country programs? c) Do findings provide information on how well integrated global and regional programs are in support of their country specific programming to increase private sector participation and to leverage dollars? **Step 10:** Sustainability issue: content analysis of KIIs on how sustainable are current government partnerships with private sector actors, likelihood of encouraging private sector participation from multi-national and local private sector companies to support achievement of CIP agreements, other pacts, other country-owned plans? Prepare findings. **Step 11:** Do findings from qualitative analysis of KII data support, confirm and/or explain findings from the overall meta-analysis outlined from Step 7? Add to the findings from Step 7 including discrepancies in findings that cannot be resolved for future action.

Question 11. How well is Feed the Future promoting policy reform at the national and regional level, including implementation?

11. How well is FTF I and promoting policy reform at the national and	19 Focus countries	Interagency FTF Policy Guide	Data mining of documents	**Step 1:** Review FTF Policy Guide Quantitative: FTFMS Data

Evaluation Questions	Units of Analysis	Data Sources	Data Collection Methods	Data Analysis Methods
regional level including implementation	**Units of Analysis** 19 Focus Aligned Regional Fieldwork BFS Aligned 5 Fieldwork countries	FTF Policy Matrices and Summaries and reports MYS for focus countries and regional programs BFS portfolio reviews of central offices promoting policy reforms: ARP, MPI. Annual reports from BFS central offices, focus, aligned and regional country programs on policy reform activities Documents from FTF Innovation Lab for Food Security Policy including their annual reports If they exist, evaluation reports covering policy implementation from the five countries selected for field work. CIPS from 5 field countries	Online survey questions on policy reform implementation KIIs in field work countries: country FTF coordinator In Missions: FGDs with Front Office Mission staff, FTF Team Lead Other KIIs in fieldwork countries: Other KIIs World Bank country rep, USDA and US Commerce/Trade representatives from donor coordinating committee	**Step 2**: Draw on Analytical Results from Evaluation Question 2 on indicators related to policy and regulatory reform for implementation progress and performance against targets disaggregated by focus, aligned and regional country programs. Highlight data from five countries selected for fieldwork. Qualitative: Structured Document reviews to identify policy agenda **Step 3**: Review MYS documents, BFS ARP and MPI documents, policy matrices to identify policy reform agenda **pursued** per focus, aligned and regional country programs. Highlight information on policy reform agenda promoted in five Focus Countries selected for field work. Review CIPs for those countries. **Step 4:** Review Policy Matrix Reports, Portfolio Reviews to identify and document data on progress in promoting reforms and to identify information on implementation. Highlight findings from five countries selected for field work and any new reforms being pursued since the initial policy reform agenda was established. Disaggregate by focus, aligned and regional country programs. **Step 5:** Compare policy reform agendas identified in Step 2 with results of Step 3 to determine follow-through on initial policy reform agendas. Document findings based on document review on progress in promoting reforms and on actual implementation. Disaggregate by focus, aligned and regional country programs.

Evaluation Questions	Units of Analysis	Data Sources	Data Collection Methods	Data Analysis Methods
	19 Focus Aligned Regional Fieldwork BFS		selected government officials involved in the agreed upon policy agenda	<u>Quantitative Analysis- Online Survey Responses</u> **Step 6:** Analyze data on responses to questions regarding policy reform promotion and implementation. Disaggregate by focus, aligned and regional country programs <u>Summary Analysis</u>
			KIIs or group interviews with FGDs per IP with policy agenda focus in the activity to include COP, M&E Manager, and key senior level technical staff on issues related to promoting implementation	**Step7:** Compare findings from document reviews on progress on promoting policy reforms and actual implementation with findings from Step 5, with findings from analysis of policy reform indicators from the FTFMS database in Step 2, and with findings from the analysis of responses from online survey data in Step 6. Do findings from each data source converge? Identify cases where there is no convergence, disaggregate by focus, aligned and regional country programs for further investigation. <u>Qualitative: KII and FGD Data</u> **Step 8** Conduct content analysis of KII and FGD data conducted in focus countries selected for field work on experiences with promoting the reform agenda with government agencies that have signed agreements related to FTF program **Step 9:** Conduct content analysis of KII data from interviews with government representatives associated with policy reforms **Step 10:** Do findings related to progress and to implementation converge between the USG partners, IPs, and government partners converge? Document, where findings converge. Document instances that do not converge for further analysis <u>Summary Analysis</u>

Evaluation Questions	Units of Analysis	Data Sources	Data Collection Methods	Data Analysis Methods
	19 Focus Aligned Regional Fieldwork BFS			**Step 11:** Compare findings from Step 10 with findings from Step 7, but specifically the analytical findings related to the five countries selected for field work. Document findings that converge and that those that do not converges. _Analysis of sustainability from KII and FGD data_ **Step 12:** Sustainability issue: Conduct content analysis of KII and FGD data on the likelihood of sustained efforts to implement policy reform agenda as outlined in CIPs including perspectives from government officials. What are the factors that promote and hinder sustained effort until policies are actually implemented?

Question 12. a) How well have Feed the Future MEL approaches achieved accountability for commitments Feed the Future has made? b. Has Feed the Future MEL system supported improved programming and b. ii how? (12 a and 12 b are treated separately)

Evaluation Questions	Units of Analysis	Data Sources	Data Collection Methods	Data Analysis Methods
12. a. How well have FTF MEL approaches achieved accountability for commitments FTF has made?	19 Focus countries Regional programs	Source documents: FTF Indicator Guide FTF M&E Guidance Series Volume 1: M&E under FTF FTF M&E Guidance Series: Frequently Asked Questions – the FTF M&E Approach FTF Five Year Goal-level Targets	KIIs in focus countries selected for field work in Missions with: AORs, AOs, FTF Coordinator/ Manager, FTF M&E Manager, Program Officer and M&E Specialist FGD interviews with each IP that include	_Qualitative: Structured Document Review_ **Step 1:** Review source documents from SPPM/MEL that outline the approach for obtaining data based on the FTF RF and causal pathways, indicators, FTF Indicators Guide, updates to FTF indicators. **Step 2:** Review FTF M&E Guidance Series, guidance for baseline data collection, and other technical guidance material developed to support and improve performance monitoring and impact and performance evaluations through baseline data collection and analysis; on-line and regional FTF M&E "classes," etc. and create a matrix of the various types and venues through which support and guidance is offered to strengthen data collection for FTF indicators.

Evaluation Questions	Units of Analysis	Data Sources	Data Collection Methods	Data Analysis Methods
	19 Focus Aligned Regional Fieldwork BFS	FTFMS data KII data FGD data on-line survey data	COP, M&E Manager and key senior technical staff On-line surveys for focus countries, regional country programs	<u>Quantitative: On-line Survey data</u> **Step 3**: Analyze responses from questions related to MEL guidance and support for performance monitoring and evaluation: clarity, utility, etc. <u>Qualitative- KIIs and FGDs data from field work</u> **Step 4:** Conduct content analysis of KII and FGD. Prepare findings from each category of individuals and groups interviewed: Mission personnel associated with FTF, Mission Program Officer and M&E specialist, FGDs with IPs on views of SPPM/MEL system for performance based FTF management and accountability, utility of guidance and support provided by MEL, and use of performance data etc. <u>Summary Analysis</u> **Step 5:** A) Do findings from the analysis of KII data support findings from the on-line survey? Where do they converge/diverge? B) Document findings from analysis of KII and FGD data provide explanations to clarify analytical results from on-line survey data? <u>Quantitative: FTFMS data</u> **Step 6:** Draw on analytical results of performance to date against targets for national goal and objective levels and for the eight IRs conducted under Evaluation Question 2 (parts a. and b). <u>Qualitative: Review of IEs and selected performance evaluations</u> **Step 7** Review contributions to understanding impact of FTF programming from IEs and selected performance evaluations

Evaluation Questions	Units of Analysis	Data Sources	Data Collection Methods	Data Analysis Methods
	19 Focus Aligned Regional Fieldwork BFS			that address basic FTF strategy. Do they provide additional evidence on progress toward meeting FTF goal level commitments? <u>Summary Analysis</u> **Step 8:** Prepare findings to respond to evaluation question based on findings from Steps 5-7
12. b.Has the FTF MEL system supported programming improved and how?	19 Focus countries 5 Fieldwork countries Regional programs	FTF Learning Agenda Update for Learning Agenda (power points) KDAD Evaluation Synthesis of Learning Agenda Evaluations KDAD website SPPM/MEL materials on feedthefuture.gov/progress and agrilinks.org for Documents/events associated with Learning Agenda (from KDAD) Annual BFS portfolio reviews of SPPM/MEL	On line surveys to 19 focus countries, regional programs regarding their use of "learning products" and FTFMS data from both Mission and BFS annual portfolio reviews as feedback loops to improve programming. **KIIs in selected field work countries** Missions: FTF coordinator, FTF M&E Specialist	<u>Qualitative: Structured Desk Review</u> **Step 1:** Create a matrix of learning products completed to date from each of the six thematic areas (includes applied research products, impact and performance evaluations, etc.). **Step 2:** Review results of research and analysis to date. How well is each topic been covered to date? To what extent are their lessons learned about technical approaches that improve outcomes based on implementation of causal pathway strategies? Actionable lessons learned? **Step 3:** Extend matrix prepared under Step 1 by adding mechanisms and vehicles for disseminating/sharing actionable lessons learned per thematic area. Include (for example), of knowledge sharing platforms, training courses, seminar series, participation in multi-donor stakeholder M&E Harmonization Group, contributions to the Global Food Security Learning Framework, etc. to determine how lessons learned, actionable lessons are shared/disseminated. **Step 4:** Is there evidence from websites and platforms, discussion groups that indicate use of learning products and their application to improve programming. Document findings.

Evaluation Questions	Units of Analysis	Data Sources	Data Collection Methods	Data Analysis Methods
	19 Focus Aligned Regional Fieldwork BFS	Online survey data KII data	Mission Program Officer FGDs per selected IPs (to include COP, DCOP, M&E Specialist, key senior technical staff)	**Step 5:** Review support provided to FTF countries to conduct baselines data. **Step 6:** Review BFS/SPPM/MEL portfolio reviews for data/discussion on use of Learning Strategy project, their utility; use of FTFMS monitoring data for improved programming. Quantitative: On-line survey data **Step 7:** Conduct analysis of data from on-line survey disaggregated by focus, aligned, and regional country programs on utility and use of learning products and how learning is accessed, etc. Which learning products and venues are most useful? Prepare findings. Qualitative: KII and FGD data **Step 8:** Conduct analysis of KII and FGD data regarding use of FTFMS data and use of learning products to improve programming. Prepare findings from each group: Mission, and IPs. Document examples of use of learning products. Summary Analysis **Step 9:** Do findings from Step 7 provide further insight to findings from on-line survey (from Step 6) with respect to utility of learning products, accessibility, and how they are used? **Step 10:** Prepare summaries of examples identified from Steps 4 and 8 on application of learning products to improve programming.

b. Draft topics to be addressed per evaluation question per key informant

FTF Program Managers

Evaluation question 3a. How well has Feed the Future focused resources on strategic and limited value chains? How have value chain approaches been applied and what have been the successes and challenges to these approaches?

1. Significant local partners – Donors, UN agency, private-sector/trade/VC organizations or associations, civil society in field visit countries
2. Significant technical contributions of the FTF framework and guide to Ag and/or food security programming.
3. Significant financial contributions of the FTF for AG and food security programming.

Evaluation question 3b. How well has the initiative focused implementation and concentrated resources in appropriate (in terms of size and agro-ecology) geographic zones? What have been successful strategies, if any?

1. Decision points in amount/types of resources, allocation to certain ZOI, etc.
2. Information on issues related to resource allocation and implementation within zones
3. Explanations for deviations in originally planned resource allocation/ implementation strategy vs. actual resource allocation and/or implementation strategy

Evaluation question 3c. To what extent has Feed the Future scaled up agriculture and nutrition interventions across the ZOI in Feed the Future Focus Countries? Are the proportions of households being reached in the ZOI sufficient to plausibly achieve the targeted impacts?

1. Opinions on likelihood of achieving targeted impacts in terms of proportions of households being reached in the ZOI
2. Factors supporting/hindering plausibility of achieving targeted impacts

USAID BFS portfolio review managers

Evaluation question 3a. How well has Feed the Future focused resources on strategic and limited value chains? How have value chain approaches been applied and what have been the successes and challenges to these approaches?

1. Significant successes in defining and rolling out FTF framework and guide

Evaluation question 3b. How well has the initiative focused implementation and concentrated resources in appropriate (in terms of size and agro-ecology) geographic zones? What have been successful strategies, if any?

1. Decision points in amount/types of resources, allocation to certain ZOI, etc.
2. Information on issues related to resource allocation and implementation within zones
3. Explanations for deviations in originally planned resource allocation/ implementation strategy vs. actual resource allocation and/or implementation strategy

Evaluation question 3c. To what extent has Feed the Future scaled up agriculture and nutrition interventions across the ZOI in Feed the Future Focus Countries? Are the proportions of households being reached in the ZOI sufficient to plausibly achieve the targeted impacts?

1. Opinions on likelihood of achieving targeted impacts in terms of proportions of households being reached in the ZOI
2. Factors supporting/hindering plausibility of achieving targeted impacts

BFS Gender Advisors

Evaluation question 5. How and to what extent have Feed the Future interventions promoted gender-inclusive agricultural sector growth and improved nutritional status of women through equitable and strategic integration of women and men in agriculture and nutrition programs?

1. Application of FTF Gender Guidelines, index, framework, and gender assessments,
2. The challenges and successes from applying guidelines and frameworks,
3. The utility of MEL Learning products related to integration of gender.

POC in USAID/Washington Food for Peace Office

1. Significant technical contributions of the FTF framework and guide for FFP programming.
2. Significant financial contributions of the FTF for FFP programming.
3. Joint FTF-FFP Action Plan for integrating/aligning programming in countries where both programs present
4. Collaboration with BFS/CSI and with Center for Resilience – how done? What is intention?

Evaluation question 3a. How well has Feed the Future focused resources on strategic and limited value chains? How have value chain approaches been applied and what have been the successes and challenges to these approaches?
> 1. Geographical overlap of FFP VC-related activities and other FFP activities.
> 2. Most significant (and beneficial) linkages between VC and FFP activities
> 3. Additional local or international resources to address food security, rural income or malnutrition that the VC-related activity drew in (leveraged)
> 4.How are FFP household beneficiaries incorporated into value chain activities? Overall strategy?
> 5. Strategies to transition/graduate FFP household beneficiaries of humanitarian assistance into households participating in value chain activities

Evaluation question 3c. To what extent has Feed the Future scaled up agriculture and nutrition interventions across the ZOI in Feed the Future Focus Countries? Are the proportions of households being reached in the ZOI sufficient to plausibly achieve the targeted impacts?
> 1. In countries where FFP and FTF are aligned: Opinion on likelihood of reaching targeted households benefiting from FFP within ZOI
> 4. In countries where FFP and FTF are aligned: Opinions on likelihood of reducing prevalence of poverty and stunting in ZOI among households benefitting from FFP to contribute to targeted goals
> 3. Factors supporting/hindering plausibility of achieving targeted impacts among FFP households in the ZOI

Evaluation question 5. How and to what extent have Feed the Future interventions promoted gender-inclusive agricultural sector growth and improved nutritional status of women through equitable and strategic integration of women and men in agriculture and nutrition programs?
> 1. Application of FTF Gender Guidelines, index, framework, and gender assessments in FFP programming for households also covered by FTF
> 2. The challenges and successes from applying guidelines and frameworks,
> 3. In countries where FFP and FTF are aligned: Contribution of households covered by FFP and FTF to targets related to inclusive agriculture sector growth

Evaluation question 6. How will have Feed the Future interventions integrated nutrition into value chain activities? Do results differ if nutrition objectives are an integral part of the value chain work? If so, how?
> 1.How does FFP help integrate nutrition interventions in locations where there is a nexus between FFP/FTF programming. Are their FFP strategies that you contribute to FTF programming?
> 2.In these instances, are nutrition interventions part of a value chain strategy that covers FFP beneficiaries?
> 3. Are nutrition interventions incorporated into the Food for Peace activities to promote agricultural productivity?

Mission Food for Peace Officer (in FTF focus countries with FFP program)

Evaluation question 3a. How well has Feed the Future focused resources on strategic and limited value chains? How have value chain approaches been applied and what have been the successes and challenges to these approaches?
> 1. Geographical overlap of FFP VC-related activities and other FFP activities
> 2. Most significant (and beneficial) linkages between VC and FFP activities
> 3. Additional local or international resources to address food security, rural income or malnutrition that the VC-related activity drew in (leveraged)
> 4.FFP beneficiaries included in one or more of the value chains? Describe strategy, how many households
> 5. Strategies to transition/graduate FFP household beneficiaries of humanitarian assistance into households participating in value chain activities

Evaluation question 3b. How well has the initiative focused implementation and concentrated resources in appropriate (in terms of size and agro-ecology) geographic zones? What have been successful strategies, if any?

    1.Does ZOI contain households benefitting from FFP?

    2.Decision points in amount/types of resources, allocation to households benefitting from FFP in ZOI , etc.

    2. Information on issues related to resource allocation and implementation within zones

    3. Explanations for deviations in originally planned resource allocation/ implementation strategy vs. actual resource allocation and/or implementation strategy

Evaluation question 3c. To what extent has Feed the Future scaled up agriculture and nutrition interventions across the ZOI in Feed the Future Focus Countries? Are the proportions of households being reached in the ZOI sufficient to plausibly achieve the targeted impacts?

    1. Opinions on likelihood of achieving targeted impacts in terms of proportions of households being reached in ZOI

    2. Factors supporting/hindering plausibility of achieving targeted impacts

    3. number of households in ZOI benefitting from both FTF and FFP activities

    4. Opinions on likehood of reducing prevalence of poverty and stunting in ZOI among households benefitting from FFP

Evaluation question 5. How and to what extent have Feed the Future interventions promoted gender-inclusive agricultural sector growth and improved nutritional status of women through equitable and strategic integration of women and men in agriculture and nutrition programs?

    1. Application of FTF Gender Guidelines, index, framework, and gender assessments in FFP programming for households also covered by FTF

    2. The challenges and successes from applying guidelines and frameworks,

    3. Contribution of households covered by FFP and FTF to targets related to inclusive agriculture sector growth

Evaluation question 6. How will have Feed the Future interventions integrated nutrition into value chain activities? Do results differ if nutrition objectives are an integral part of the value chain work? If so, how?

    1.Integration of nutrition interventions in locations where there is a nexus between FFP/FTF programming. H

    2.In these instances, are nutrition interventions part of a value chain strategy that covers FFP beneficiaries?

    3. Are nutrition interventions incorporated into the Food for Peace activities to promote agricultural productivity?

C/AORs for centrally managed program with HICD component

Evaluation question 4. How and to what extent have Feed the Future interventions, both Mission - and centrally managed helped build human and institutional capacities for the agricultural and nutrition/health sectors?

    1. The extent to which initial targets differed from actual results and why? Did results differ by sector (nutrition vs. agriculture)? How often did USAID review these data, how did USAID use these data, what actions were taken to shape programs based on these data?

    2. Did the process for HICD programming differ between agriculture and agricultural activities, if yes explain, how did USAID guide implementers on these expectations?

    3. Was there a mechanism for coordination to avoid duplication of effort at the country level (i.e. training the same people vs. complementary training efforts) -describe it. Who initiated it and ran it?

    4. Did HICD efforts under FTF result in any novel approaches to HICD beyond what USAID had been supporting before FTF? Explain.

    5. Describe successes/challenges/lessons learned of HICD implementation under FTF.

Implementing partners for 5 centrally managed activities with HICD components

Evaluation question 4. How and to what extent have Feed the Future interventions, both Mission - and centrally managed helped build human and institutional capacities for the agricultural and nutrition/health sectors?

    1. The extent to which initial targets differed from actual results and why? Did results differ by sector (nutrition vs. agriculture) How often did you review these data with USAID, how were these data used in

program management?

2. Did the process for HICD programming differ between nutrition and agricultural activities, how, what did your organization do to make the adjustments necessary to meet expectations for both?

3. Was there a mechanism for coordination to avoid duplication of effort at the country level (i.e. training the same people vs. complementary training efforts). Describe it. Who initiated it and ran it?

4. Did you undertake any activities under FTF that were novel compared to previous programming/models that you were using prior to FTF? Did FTF spur you to act any differently from your work pre-FTF? Examples?

5. Describe successes/challenges/lessons learned of HICD implementation under FTF.

In Country Mission FTF Coordinator/ Manager

Evaluation question 1. How well have strategies and the implementation of programs followed the Results Framework and the causal pathways identified therein?

1. Extent to which Mission FTF portfolio and individual projects and activities are based on the FTF RF and strategy based on causal pathways

2. Does project and activity implementation follow the FTF RF and strategy? Have there been any strategic changes? Which projects/activities

3. (If strategic changes in implementation) have changes been documented? Explanations for strategy change and effect of doing so.

Evaluation question 3a. How well has Feed the Future focused resources on strategic and limited value chains? How have value chain approaches been applied and what have been the successes and challenges to these approaches?

1. Explanations for deviations in originally planned resource allocation/ implementation strategy vs. actual resource allocation and/or implementation strategy

2. What have been factors enabling meeting/exceeding targets within each zone?

3. What have been factors hindering meeting/exceeding targets within each zone?

Evaluation question 3b. How well has the initiative focused implementation and concentrated resources in appropriate (in terms of size and agro-ecology) geographic zones? What have been successful strategies, if any?

1. Opinions on likelihood of achieving targeted impacts in terms of proportions of households being reached in the ZOI

2. Factors supporting/hindering plausibility of achieving targeted impacts

Evaluation question 3c. To what extent has Feed the Future scaled up agriculture and nutrition interventions across the ZOI in Feed the Future Focus Countries? Are the proportions of households being reached in the ZOI sufficient to plausibly achieve the targeted impacts?

1. Application of FTF Gender Guidelines, index, framework, and gender assessments

2. The challenges and successes from applying guidelines and frameworks

3. The utility of MEL Learning products related to integration of gender.

Evaluation question 5. How and to what extent have Feed the Future interventions promoted gender-inclusive agricultural sector growth and improved nutritional status of women through equitable and strategic integration of women and men in agriculture and nutrition programs?

1. Application of FTF Gender Policy and ADS Guidelines, and gender assessments

2. The challenges and successes from applying guidelines and frameworks

3. The utility of MEL Learning products related to integration of gender.

Evaluation question 6. How will have Feed the Future interventions integrated nutrition into value chain activities? Do results differ if nutrition objectives are an integral part of the value chain work? If so, how?

1. Process that led to the design of the VC and their consideration of nutrition in that process.

2. Review data on VC and nutrition, request comments/feedback on successes/challenges/lessons learned

Mission FTF AORs/CORS

Evaluation question 1. How well have strategies and the implementation of programs followed the Results Framework and the causal pathways identified therein?

1. Explanations for change in strategy/implementation based on FTF causal pathways
2. Effect of changes in outcomes
3. Documentation of changes
4. Challenges to implementing FTF RF strategy based on its causal pathways

Evaluation question 3b. How well has the initiative focused implementation and concentrated resources in appropriate (in terms of size and agro-ecology) geographic zones? What have been successful strategies, if any?
1. Decision points in amount/types of resources, allocation to certain ZOI, etc.
2. Explanations for deviations in originally planned resource allocation/ implementation strategy vs. actual resource allocation and/or implementation strategy

Evaluation question 3c. To what extent has Feed the Future scaled up agriculture and nutrition interventions across the ZOI in Feed the Future Focus Countries? Are the proportions of households being reached in the ZOI sufficient to plausibly achieve the targeted impacts?
1. Opinions on likelihood of achieving targeted impacts in terms of proportions of households being reached in the ZOI
2. Factors supporting/hindering plausibility of achieving targeted impacts

Evaluation question 5. How and to what extent have Feed the Future interventions promoted gender-inclusive agricultural sector growth and improved nutritional status of women through equitable and strategic integration of women and men in agriculture and nutrition programs?
1. Application of FTF Gender Guidelines, index, framework, and gender assessments
2. The challenges and successes from applying guidelines and frameworks
3. The utility of MEL Learning products related to integration of gender.

Mission Gender Advisor
Evaluation question 5. How and to what extent have Feed the Future interventions promoted gender-inclusive agricultural sector growth and improved nutritional status of women through equitable and strategic integration of women and men in agriculture and nutrition programs?
1. Application of FTF Gender Guidelines, index, framework, and gender assessments
2. The challenges and successes from applying guidelines and frameworks
3. The utility of MEL Learning products related to integration of gender.

Evaluation question 3c. To what extent has Feed the Future scaled up agriculture and nutrition interventions across the ZOI in Feed the Future Focus Countries? Are the proportions of households being reached in the ZOI sufficient to plausibly achieve the targeted impacts?
1. Opinions on likelihood of achieving targeted impacts in terms of proportions of households being reached in the ZOI
2. Factors supporting/hindering plausibility of achieving targeted impacts

FGDs per IP (COP, senior technical staff, IP M&E Manager)
Evaluation question 1. How well have strategies and the implementation of programs followed the Results Framework and the causal pathways identified therein?
1. Rationale and factors promoting change in strategy/strategy implementation - documented?
2. Challenges to strategy design and implementation based on FTF RF and strategy based on causal pathways
3. Describe changes. What effect to date on achieving outcomes?

Evaluation question 3a. How well has Feed the Future focused resources on strategic and limited value chains? How have value chain approaches been applied and what have been the successes and challenges to these approaches?
1. Quick validation of the VC approach as per the topology developed by the FTF Eval Team
2. Does the VC design and implementation reflect CAADP (Africa) and CIP priorities, if not, why not?
3. How their activity complements (addresses critical gaps) or supplements (augment) other VC work?
4. Adjustments to the ZOI or locations within the ZOI
5. Linkages to other FTF activities within the ZOI

6. Three/four key successes of your VC activity

7. What factors have been key to each success

8. How FTF framework and/or guide contributed to these successes

9. Three/four challenges you faced or continue to face in implementing the VC activity

10. How would you modify the design or implementation in the future to address these challenges?

11. Additional local or international resources to address VC needs, rural income, employment or malnutrition that the VC activity drew in (leveraged)

Evaluation question 3b. How well has the initiative focused implementation and concentrated resources in appropriate (in terms of size and agro-ecology) geographic zones? What have been successful strategies, if any?

1. Explanations for deviations in originally planned resource allocation/ implementation strategy vs. actual resource allocation and/or implementation strategy

2. What have been factors enabling meeting/exceeding targets within each zone?

3. What have been factors hindering meeting/exceeding targets within each zone?

4. M&E Systems ability to capture factors affecting ability to meet targets

5: M&E System's ability to capture resource allocation/concentration in zones

Evaluation question 3c. To what extent has Feed the Future scaled up agriculture and nutrition interventions across the ZOI in Feed the Future Focus Countries? Are the proportions of households being reached in the ZOI sufficient to plausibly achieve the targeted impacts?

1. Opinions on likelihood of achieving targeted impacts in terms of proportions of households being reached in the ZOI

2. Factors supporting/hindering plausibility of achieving targeted impacts

Evaluation question 5. How and to what extent have Feed the Future interventions promoted gender-inclusive agricultural sector growth and improved nutritional status of women through equitable and strategic integration of women and men in agriculture and nutrition programs?

1. Application of FTF Gender Guidelines, index, framework, and gender assessments

2. The challenges and successes from applying guidelines and frameworks

3. The utility of MEL Learning products related to integration of gender.

Evaluation question 6. How will have Feed the Future interventions integrated nutrition into value chain activities? Do results differ if nutrition objectives are an integral part of the value chain work? If so, how?

1. Process that led to the design of the VC and their consideration of nutrition in that process.

2. Review data on VC and nutrition, request comments/feedback on successes/challenges/lessons learned

USG in country rep: USDA, USG in country rep: Trade Commerce

Evaluation question 3c. To what extent has Feed the Future scaled up agriculture and nutrition interventions across the ZOI in Feed the Future Focus Countries? Are the proportions of households being reached in the ZOI sufficient to plausibly achieve the targeted impacts?

1. Opinions on likelihood of achieving targeted impacts in terms of proportions of households being reached in the ZOI

2. Factors supporting/hindering plausibility of achieving targeted impacts

FTF Team Lead

Evaluation question 3c. To what extent has Feed the Future scaled up agriculture and nutrition interventions across the ZOI in Feed the Future Focus Countries? Are the proportions of households being reached in the ZOI sufficient to plausibly achieve the targeted impacts?

1. Opinions on likelihood of achieving targeted impacts in terms of proportions of households being reached in the ZOI

2. Factors supporting/hindering plausibility of achieving targeted impacts

Evaluation question 3a. How well has Feed the Future focused resources on strategic and limited value chains? How have value chain approaches been applied and what have been the successes and challenges to these approaches?

1. Significant technical contributions of the FTF framework and guide to strategy and program development.
2. Significant local partners – Donors, UN agency, private-sector/trade/VC organizations or associations, civil society
4. New partners or initiatives created in response to FTF activities/resources
5. Quick validation of the VC approach as per the topology developed by the FTF Eval Team
6. Does the VC design and implementation reflect CAADP (Africa) and CIP priorities, if not, why not?
7. How the activity complements (addresses critical gaps) or supplements (augment) other VC work?
8. Adjustments to the ZOI or locations within the ZOI
9. Linkages to other FTF activities within the ZOI
10. Three/four key successes of your VC activity
11. What factors have been key to each success
12. How FTF framework and/or guide contributed to these successes
13. Three/four challenges you faced or continue to face in implementing the VC activity
14. How would you modify the design or implementation in the future to address these challenges?
15. Additional local or international resources to address VC needs, rural income or malnutrition that the VC activity drew in (leveraged)

Government partners: Ministry of Ag., Ministry of Livestock, Min of Health, Min of Fisheries, etc.

Evaluation question 3b. How well has the initiative focused implementation and concentrated resources in appropriate (in terms of size and agro-ecology) geographic zones? What have been successful strategies, if any?

1. The appropriateness of the resource allocation/implementation strategies within each zone
2. Factors that enable and hinder achieving targets

Evaluation question 4. How and to what extent have Feed the Future interventions, both Mission - and centrally managed helped build human and institutional capacities for the agricultural and nutrition/health sectors?

1. Has your operating unit benefitted from HICD activities under USAID's FTF initiative?
2. Give some examples of HICD activities that you are aware of.
3. How did USAID choose who would be recipient of HICD? Was your unit/Ministry involved? How? (country ownership cross walk) What mechanisms were in place to ensure transparency of selection of recipients for HICD (efficiency, transparency)?
4. What mechanisms are in place to ensure that your ministry is able to continue to benefit from this assistance in a long term way (sustainability)?
5. Successes/ challenges/ lessons learned from this experience with USAID

Focus Group for HICD: Program Officer, FTF Team Lead, C/AORs of Mission managed awards, Implementing partners of top 2-3 awards (dollar value) with HICD activities

Evaluation question 4. How and to what extent have Feed the Future interventions, both Mission - and centrally managed helped build human and institutional capacities for the agricultural and nutrition/health sectors?

1. The extent to which initial targets differed from actual results and why? Did results differ by sector (nutrition vs. agriculture)? How often did you review these data (internally in USAID and with IP)? How were these data used in program management?
2. Did the process for HICD programming differ between nutrition and agricultural activities, how, what did your organization do to make the adjustments necessary to meet expectations for both?
3. Was there a mechanism for coordination to avoid duplication of effort between projects and among development projects (across the donor spectrum) at the country/beneficiary level (i.e. training the same people vs complementary training efforts). Describe it. Who initiated it and ran it?
4. Did you undertake any activities under FTF that were novel compared to previous programming/models that you were using prior to FTF? Did FTF spur you to act any differently from your work pre-FTF?
5. Describe successes/challenges of HICD implementation under FTF.
6. How have HICD activities contributed to broader FTF outcomes of interest? Which has it impacted more?
7. What is the Mission/IPs doing to ensure sustainability of HICD activities?

Focus Group: Each IP to include COP/DCOP, M&E Specialist, Senior Technical Directors

Evaluation question 1. How well have strategies and the implementation of programs followed the Results Framework and the causal pathways identified therein?

    1. Rationale and factors promoting change in strategy/strategy implementation - documented?

    2. Challenges to strategy design and implementation based on FTF RF and strategy based on causal pathways

    3.Describe changes, what effect to date on achieving outcomes?

Nutrition specialist-Health or FTF team

Evaluation question 1. How well have strategies and the implementation of programs followed the Results Framework and the causal pathways identified therein?

    1. Rationale and factors promoting change in strategy/strategy implementation - documented?

    2. Challenges to strategy design and implementation based on FTF RF and strategy based on causal pathways

    3.Describe changes. What effect to date on achieving outcomes?

Evaluation question 5. How and to what extent have Feed the Future interventions promoted gender-inclusive agricultural sector growth and improved nutritional status of women through equitable and strategic integration of women and men in agriculture and nutrition programs?

    1. Application of FTF Gender Guidelines, index, framework, and gender assessments

    2. Challenges and successes from applying guidelines and frameworks

    3. The utility of MEL Learning products related to integration of gender.

Evaluation question 6. How will have Feed the Future interventions integrated nutrition into value chain activities? Do results differ if nutrition objectives are an integral part of the value chain work? If so, how?

    1. Process that led to the design of the VC and their consideration of nutrition in that process.

    2. Was nutritionist involved? How, at what point in the process, how did they contribute?

    3. Review data on VC and nutrition, request comments/feedback on successes/challenges/lessons learned

Mission Ag. Officer

Evaluation question 3a. How well has Feed the Future focused resources on strategic and limited value chains? How have value chain approaches been applied and what have been the successes and challenges to these approaches?

    1. Significant technical contributions of the FTF framework and guide to strategy and program development.

    2. Significant local partners – Donors, UN agency, private-sector/trade/VC organizations or associations, civil society

    4. New partners or initiatives created in response to FTF activities/resources

    5. Does the VC design and implementation reflect CAADP (Africa) and CIP priorities, if not, why not?

    6. How the activity complements (addresses critical gaps) or supplements (augment) other VC work?

    7. Adjustments to the ZOI or locations within the ZOI

    8. Linkages to other FTF activities within the ZOI

    9. Three/four key successes of your VC activity

    10. What factors have been key to each success

    11. How FTF framework and/or guide contributed to these successes

    12. Three/four challenges you faced or continue to face in implementing the VC activity

    13. How would you modify the design or implementation in the future to address these challenges?

    14. Additional local or international resources to address VC needs, rural income or malnutrition that the VC activity drew in (leveraged)

GHFS Coordinator Washington, DC

Evaluation question 11. How well is Feed the Future identifying and promoting policy reform at the national and regional level, including implementation of policy reform? Which kinds of regional policy interventions have been the most effective at contributing to bilateral impacts and why?

    1. Views on how well WOG approach is doing in identifying and promoting policy reforms to help country programs, policy implementation successes to date

2.Views on how well USAID regional country programs are able to promote policy reforms and their implementation successes to date that contribute to bilateral country impacts

3. Views on how well Country FTF coordinator in facilitating a unified WOG approach to identifying and promoting policy reforms consistent with government CIP agreement

BFS Managers/Lead per Research agenda

Evaluation question 9. How effectively is Feed the Future marshaling relevant capacities in U.S. and global research organizations? How well are Feed the Future-supported research activities designed to address major global challenges and spur agricultural development across initiative Focus Countries? To what extent are research products being disseminated and/or commercialized?

  1. Information regarding the types of research capacities solicited from the research organizations
  2. Variation in types of capacities of US vs. Global research organizations
  3. Reasons for utilizing the particular research organizations identified
  4. Gaps in research capacities not filled by any of the research organizations
  5. Reasons for commissioning the particular types of research and post-research activities conducted
  6. What forms of research products dissemination/commercialization are used? Promoted? Discouraged?
  7. Factors that support and hinder decision to disseminate research products

USAID FTF Deputy Coordinator for Development

Evaluation question 11. How well is Feed the Future identifying and promoting policy reform at the national and regional level, including implementation of policy reform? Which kinds of regional policy interventions have been the most effective at contributing to bilateral impacts and why?

  1. Based on annual FTF portfolio reviews, how well is FTF doing at promoting implementation of policy reforms as outlined in MYS documents, CIPs
  2. Common challenges across country and regional programs? Specific approaches related to success in policy implementation
  3.Effect of successful policy reform implementation, and lagging policy reform implementation that portfolio reviews have identified to date. Evidence to support those conclusions sufficient?
  4.Effectiveness to date of regional policy reforms promoted by regional country programs and contributions to bilateral program outcomes - views based on FTF portfolio reviews from regional and focus country programs

US Dept. of State FTF Deputy Coordinator for Diplomacy

Evaluation question 11. How well is Feed the Future identifying and promoting policy reform at the national and regional level, including implementation of policy reform? Which kinds of regional policy interventions have been the most effective at contributing to bilateral impacts and why?

  1. Based on annual FTF portfolio reviews, how well is FTF doing at promoting implementation of policy reforms as outlined in MYS documents, CIPs
  2. Common challenges across country and regional programs? Specific approaches related to success in policy implementation
  3.Effect of successful policy reform implementation, and lagging policy reform implementation that portfolio reviews have identified to date. Evidence to support those conclusions sufficient?
  4.Effectiveness to date of regional policy reforms promoted by regional country programs and contributions to bilateral program outcomes - views based on FTF portfolio reviews from regional and focus country programs
  Norman Borlaug Commemorative Research Initiative (NBCRI) Rep
  7. The effectiveness of the initiative's focus on country ownership. How well has Feed the Future invested in country-owned plans that support results-based programs and partnerships?
  8. What has been Feed the Future's contribution to influencing and leveraging multi-lateral institutions and initiatives, thus shaping the evolving food security landscape, which will, in turn affect the future form and function of the initiative?
  9. How effectively is Feed the Future marshaling relevant capacities in U.S. and global research organizations? How well are Feed the Future-supported research activities designed to address major global

challenges and spur agricultural development across initiative Focus Countries? To what extent are research products being disseminated and/or commercialized?

11. How well is Feed the Future identifying and promoting policy reform at the national and regional level, including implementation of policy reform? Which kinds of regional policy interventions have been the most effective at contributing to bilateral impacts and why?

12. How well has Feed the Future's system and approaches for monitoring, evaluations, and learning (MEL) facilitated requisite levels of accountability and learning? How well have Feed the Future MEL approaches achieved accountability for commitments Feed the Future has made? Has Feed the Future MEL supported improved programming and how?

Feed the Future Innovation Labs

Evaluation question 11. How well is Feed the Future identifying and promoting policy reform at the national and regional level, including implementation of policy reform? Which kinds of regional policy interventions have been the most effective at contributing to bilateral impacts and why?

1. Capacity in which the organization supports FTF research activities
2. Global challenges being addressed by research activities
3. Any gaps in research activities
4. Forms of research products dissemination/ commercialization within FTF realm and beyond

CGIAR Rep.

Evaluation question 7. The effectiveness of the initiative's focus on country ownership. How well has Feed the Future invested in country-owned plans that support results-based programs and partnerships?

1. New streams of funding created for G8 agriculture and nutrition agenda in response to FTF political or financial contributions
2. New partners or initiatives created in response to FTF activities/guidance/resources
3. Significant technical contributions of FTF funded activities
4. Important technical or financial gaps related to work on AG/Food Security research addressed through FTF technical or financial contributions
5. Evidence new linkages between AG research and field-level program implementation (e.g., FTF implementing partner work with farmers)

Evaluation question 8. What has been Feed the Future's contribution to influencing and leveraging multi-lateral institutions and initiatives, thus shaping the evolving food security landscape, which will, in turn affect the future form and function of the initiative?

1. New streams of funding created for G8 agriculture and nutrition agenda in response to FTF political or financial contributions
2. New partners or initiatives created in response to FTF activities/guidance/resources
3. Significant technical contributions of FTF funded activities
4. Important technical or financial gaps related to work on AG/Food Security research addressed through FTF technical or financial contributions
5. Evidence new linkages between AG research and field-level program implementation (e.g., FTF implementing partner work with farmers)

Evaluation question 9. How effectively is Feed the Future marshaling relevant capacities in U.S. and global research organizations? How well are Feed the Future-supported research activities designed to address major global challenges and spur agricultural development across initiative Focus Countries? To what extent are research products being disseminated and/or commercialized?

1. Capacity in which the organization supports FTF research activities
2. Global challenges being addressed by research activities
3. Any gaps in research activities
4. Forms of research products dissemination/ commercialization within FTF realm and beyond

Global Agriculture and Food Security Program (GAFSP) Rep., New Alliance for Food Security and Nutrition (NA) Rep., G8

Evaluation question 7. The effectiveness of the initiative's focus on country ownership. How well has Feed the Future invested in country-owned plans that support results-based programs and partnerships?

     1. Significant FTF technical contributions to the GAFSP partnership

     2. Significant FTF financial contributions to the GAFSP partnership and, in particular, those facilitating strategic programming

     3. New streams of funding created for GAFSP in response to FTF engagement

     4. New partners or initiatives created in response to FTF activities/resources

     5. New areas of programming initiated due to FTF technical or financial leadership

Evaluation question 8. What has been Feed the Future's contribution to influencing and leveraging multi-lateral institutions and initiatives, thus shaping the evolving food security landscape, which will, in turn affect the future form and function of the initiative?

     1. Significant FTF technical contributions to the GAFSP partnership

     2. Significant FTF financial contributions to the GAFSP partnership and, in particular, those facilitating strategic programming

     3. New streams of funding created for GAFSP in response to FTF engagement

     4. New partners or initiatives created in response to FTF activities/resources

     5. New areas of programming initiated due to FTF technical or financial leadership

Mission FTF Team Lead

Evaluation question 9. How effectively is Feed the Future marshaling relevant capacities in U.S. and global research organizations? How well are Feed the Future-supported research activities designed to address major global challenges and spur agricultural development across initiative Focus Countries? To what extent are research products being disseminated and/or commercialized?

     1. Information regarding the types of research capacities solicited from the research organizations

     2. Variation in types of capacities of US vs. Global research organizations

     3. Reasons for utilizing the particular research organizations identified

     4. Gaps in research capacities not filled by any of the research organizations

     5. Reasons for commissioning the particular types of research and post-research activities conducted

     6. What forms of research products dissemination/commercialization are used? Promoted? Discouraged?

     7. Factors that support and hinder decision to disseminate research products

Evaluation question 11. How well is Feed the Future identifying and promoting policy reform at the national and regional level, including implementation of policy reform? Which kinds of regional policy interventions have been the most effective at contributing to bilateral impacts and why?

     1. Views on how well Mission and WOG representatives in country are doing in promoting policy reform agenda outline in CIP, and effectiveness of their approaches to promote government implementation. USAID Mission and other USG reps coordinating?

     2. Implementation successes to date, challenges, how has FTF been able to foster government implementation?

     3. Effects of either lagging or successful implementation of policy reforms on country program progress in achieving FTF goals and outcomes?

     4. How well does FTF coordinate with donor coordination committee with respect to policy reform promotion and implementation

     5. Views on effect of cross-border policy reforms implemented to date on country program FTF outcomes and goals

Mission FTF AORs/CORS

Evaluation question 9. How effectively is Feed the Future marshaling relevant capacities in U.S. and global research organizations? How well are Feed the Future-supported research activities designed to address major global challenges and spur agricultural development across initiative Focus Countries? To what extent are research products being disseminated and/or commercialized?

1. Reasons for utilizing the particular research organizations identified
2. Reasons for commissioning the particular types of research and post-research activities conducted
3. What forms of research products dissemination/commercialization are used? Promoted? Discouraged?
4. Factors that support and hinder decision to disseminate research products

Mission Gender Advisor

Evaluation question 11. How well is Feed the Future identifying and promoting policy reform at the national and regional level, including implementation of policy reform? Which kinds of regional policy interventions have been the most effective at contributing to bilateral impacts and why?

1. Identification and implementation of policies affecting inclusion of women in ag activities, e.g. access to loans
2. effectiveness of approaches used to promote necessary reforms and progress to date

Evaluation question12. How well has Feed the Future's system and approaches for monitoring, evaluations, and learning (MEL) facilitated requisite levels of accountability and learning? How well have Feed the Future MEL approaches achieved accountability for commitments Feed the Future has made? Has Feed the Future MEL supported improved programming and how?

1. Utility and effective use of Gender Integration Framework, Women's Empowerment in Agriculture Index, FTF M&E Guidance Series with respect to gender, FTF Indicator handbook
2. How well IPs are doing collecting FTF indicator data on gender disaggregated basis, indicator data from WEAI, and other gender specific indicators
3. Use of data from these indicators to improve program - evidence? How can this be improved?
4. Utility and use of BFS supported Learning and Research products related to gender and accessibility of products

Mission FTF M&E Manager

Evaluation question 7. The effectiveness of the initiative's focus on country ownership. How well has Feed the Future invested in country-owned plans that support results-based programs and partnerships?

1. FTF activities that have increased coverage, quality, analysis and/or reporting of agriculture/food security/nutrition data and information
2. FTF activities most significant successes (contribution to improved information systems performance)
3. Remaining significant challenges to working within the agriculture and nutrition information systems.
4. Examples of how FTF has leveraged additional resources for the local agriculture and nutrition information systems
5. Examples of how data and/or information from the AG and/or nutrition information system was used for government policy analysis, planning or programming decisions
6. Examples of how data and/or information from the AG and/or nutrition information system were used at the community, farm or household level to better manage food security.

Evaluation question 8. What has been Feed the Future's contribution to influencing and leveraging multi-lateral institutions and initiatives, thus shaping the evolving food security landscape, which will, in turn affect the future form and function of the initiative?

1. FTF activities that have increased coverage, quality, analysis and/or reporting of agriculture/food security/nutrition data and information
2. FTF activities most significant successes (contribution to improved information systems performance)
3. Remaining significant challenges to working within the agriculture and nutrition information systems.
4. Examples of how FTF has leveraged additional resources for the local agriculture and nutrition information systems
5. Examples of how data and/or information from the AG and/or nutrition information system was used for government policy analysis, planning or programming decisions
6. Examples of how data and/or information from the AG and/or nutrition information system were used at the community, farm or household level to better manage food security.

Evaluation question12. How well has Feed the Future's system and approaches for monitoring, evaluations, and learning (MEL) facilitated requisite levels of accountability and learning? How well have Feed the Future MEL approaches achieved accountability for commitments Feed the Future has made? Has Feed the Future MEL supported improved programming and how?

> FGD that includes the Mission FTF M&E Manager, Program Officer, M&E Specialists to ask questions regarding the FTF performance monitoring system.

IP (COP, senior technical staff, IP M&E Manager)

Evaluation question 7. The effectiveness of the initiative's focus on country ownership. How well has Feed the Future invested in country-owned plans that support results-based programs and partnerships?

> 1. FTF activities that have increased coverage, quality, analysis and/or reporting of agriculture/food security/nutrition data and information
> 2. FTF activities most significant successes (contribution to improved information systems performance)
> 3. Remaining significant challenges to working within the agriculture and nutrition information systems.
> 4. Examples of how FTF has leveraged additional resources for the local agriculture and nutrition information systems
> 5. Examples of how data and/or information from the AG and/or nutrition information system was used for government policy analysis, planning or programming decisions
> 6. Examples of how data and/or information from the AG and/or nutrition information system were used at the community, farm or household level to better manage food security.

Evaluation question 8. What has been Feed the Future's contribution to influencing and leveraging multi-lateral institutions and initiatives, thus shaping the evolving food security landscape, which will, in turn affect the future form and function of the initiative?

> 1. FTF activities that have increased coverage, quality, analysis and/or reporting of agriculture/food security/nutrition data and information
> 2. FTF activities most significant successes (contribution to improved information systems performance)
> 3. Remaining significant challenges to working within the agriculture and nutrition information systems.
> 4. Examples of how FTF has leveraged additional resources for the local agriculture and nutrition information systems
> 5. Examples of how data and/or information from the AG and/or nutrition information system was used for government policy analysis, planning or programming decisions
> 6. Examples of how data and/or information from the AG and/or nutrition information system were used at the community, farm or household level to better manage food security.

Evaluation question 9. How effectively is Feed the Future marshaling relevant capacities in U.S. and global research organizations? How well are Feed the Future-supported research activities designed to address major global challenges and spur agricultural development across initiative Focus Countries? To what extent are research products being disseminated and/or commercialized?

> 1. Information regarding the types of research capacities solicited from the research organizations
> 2. Variation in types of capacities of US vs. Global research organizations
> 3. Reasons for utilizing the particular research organizations identified
> 4. Gaps in research capacities not filled by any of the research organizations
> 5. Reasons for commissioning the particular types of research and post-research activities conducted
> 6. What forms of research products dissemination/commercialization are used? Promoted? Discouraged?
> 7. Factors that support and hinder decision to disseminate research products

Evaluation question 12. How well has Feed the Future's system and approaches for monitoring, evaluations, and learning (MEL) facilitated requisite levels of accountability and learning? How well have Feed the Future MEL approaches achieved accountability for commitments Feed the Future has made? Has Feed the Future MEL supported improved programming and how?

> 1. Clarity, utility and application of guidance from BS/SPPM/MEL on M&E approach, FTF Indicator Guide, FTF M&E Guidance Series, Women's Empowerment in Agriculture Index in the Mission FTF Portfolio overall, and in specific projects/activities

2. Confusion about FTF indicator definitions, data collection and analytical procedures? Received assistance from third party M&E project to clarify?

3. Utility of indicators for measuring effectiveness of strategies based on causal pathways and outputs, sub-IRs, IRs, objectives from the FTF RF…what's missing? What isn't working

4. How well is this set of FTF indicators promoting results-based management to achieve FTF goals and objective in your project? Does the FTF M&E system help promote achievement of outcomes and goals in Mission FTF activities and projects

5. Accessibility to, and utility and use of FTF BFS supported research and learning products, actionable lessons learned to Mission FTF program. Use of products, webinar events, etc.?

6. Use of data provided to Mission FTF portfolio reviews, and extent of feeding back performance to date on key indicators to improve activity/project performance

7. Examples of how data analysis from FTF indicators, research and learning products and events have been used to improve outcomes to date in your activity/project

Individuals from Universities/Research Institutes

<u>Evaluation question 9.</u> How effectively is Feed the Future marshaling relevant capacities in U.S. and global research organizations? How well are Feed the Future-supported research activities designed to address major global challenges and spur agricultural development across initiative Focus Countries? To what extent are research products being disseminated and/or commercialized?

1. Capacity in which the organization supports FTF research activities
2. Global challenges being addressed by research activities
3. Any gaps in research activities
4. Forms of research products dissemination/ commercialization within FTF realm and beyond

MCC Rep.

<u>Evaluation question 7.</u> The effectiveness of the initiative's focus on country ownership. How well has Feed the Future invested in country-owned plans that support results-based programs and partnerships?

1. Significant FTF political, technical and/or financial contributions to the G8 poverty and nutrition priorities and goals (e.g., MDGs).
2. New streams of funding created for MDG agriculture and nutrition agenda in response to FTF engagement
3. New partners or initiatives created in response to FTF activities/resources
4. New streams of funding created for the MCC country program in response to FTF engagement
5. New partners or initiatives created for the MCC country program in response to FTF activities/resources
6. New areas of programming initiated that support the MCC country program due to FTF technical or financial leadership

<u>Evaluation question 8.</u> What has been Feed the Future's contribution to influencing and leveraging multi-lateral institutions and initiatives, thus shaping the evolving food security landscape, which will, in turn affect the future form and function of the initiative?

1. Significant FTF political, technical and/or financial contributions to the G8 poverty and nutrition priorities and goals (e.g., MDGs).
2. New streams of funding created for MDG agriculture and nutrition agenda in response to FTF engagement
3. New partners or initiatives created in response to FTF activities/resources
4. New streams of funding created for the MCC country program in response to FTF engagement
5. New partners or initiatives created for the MCC country program in response to FTF activities/resources
6. New areas of programming initiated that support the MCC country program due to FTF technical or financial leadership

3rd Party M&E IPs

<u>Evaluation question 12.</u> How well has Feed the Future's system and approaches for monitoring, evaluations, and learning (MEL) facilitated requisite levels of accountability and learning? How well have Feed the Future MEL approaches achieved accountability for commitments Feed the Future has made? Has Feed the Future MEL supported improved programming and how?

1. Clarity, utility and application of guidance from BS/SPPM/MEL on M&E approach, FTF Indicator Guide, FTF M&E Guidance Series, Women's Empowerment in Agriculture Index in the Mission FTF Portfolio overall, and in specific projects/activities
2. Confusion among IPs about FTF indicator definitions, data collection and analytical procedures? Are IPs contributing to same indicators using same definitions/approaches to data collection and analysis?
3. Utility of indicators for measuring effectiveness of strategies based on causal pathways and outputs, sub-IRs, IRs, objectives from the FTF RF - what's missing? What isn't working
4. How well is this set of indicators promoting results-based monitoring and accountability to achieve FTF objectives and goals? Does the FTF M&E system promote achievement of outcomes and goals in Mission FTF activities and projects
5. Accessibility to, and utility and use of FTF BFS supported research and learning products, actionable lessons learned to Mission FTF program?
6. Use of data in Mission FTF portfolio reviews, and extent of feeding back performance to date on key indicators to improve activity/project performance

World Bank Country Rep., Other Donors working within same country/sector and/or ZOI

Evaluation question 7. The effectiveness of the initiative's focus on country ownership. How well has Feed the Future invested in country-owned plans that support results-based programs and partnerships?
1. Ease of collaboration with FTF in planning and implementation
2. New areas of programming created in response to FTF engagement
3. New partners or initiatives created in response to FTF activities/resources

Evaluation question 8. What has been Feed the Future's contribution to influencing and leveraging multi-lateral institutions and initiatives, thus shaping the evolving food security landscape, which will, in turn affect the future form and function of the initiative?
1. Ease of collaboration with FTF in planning and implementation
2. New areas of programming created in response to FTF engagement
3. New partners or initiatives created in response to FTF activities/resources

Regional Development Banks

Evaluation question 7. The effectiveness of the initiative's focus on country ownership. How well has Feed the Future invested in country-owned plans that support results-based programs and partnerships?
1. New streams of funding created in response to FTF engagement
2. New partners or initiatives created in response to FTF activities/resources
3. New areas of programming initiated due to FTF technical or financial leadership
4. Important technical or financial gaps related to work on AG/Food Security addressed through FTF technical or financial contributions

Evaluation question 8. What has been Feed the Future's contribution to influencing and leveraging multi-lateral institutions and initiatives, thus shaping the evolving food security landscape, which will, in turn affect the future form and function of the initiative?
1. New streams of funding created in response to FTF engagement
2. New partners or initiatives created in response to FTF activities/resources
3. New areas of programming initiated due to FTF technical or financial leadership
4. Important technical or financial gaps related to work on AG/Food Security addressed through FTF technical or financial contributions

FGD with (Mission FTF Team Lead, Mission Director, Program Officer, other Mission leads involved in policy reform agenda)

Evaluation question 11. How well is Feed the Future identifying and promoting policy reform at the national and regional level, including implementation of policy reform? Which kinds of regional policy interventions have been the most effective at contributing to bilateral impacts and why?

1.Views on how well Mission specifically and other WOG representatives in country are doing in promoting policy reform agenda outline in CIP, and effectiveness of their approaches to promote government implementation. USAID Mission and other USG reps coordinating?

2. Implementation successes to date, challenges, how has FTF program been able to foster government implementation? What approaches?

3. Effects of either lagging or successful implementation of policy reforms on country program progress in achieving FTF goals and outcomes?

4. The role of specific FTF activities/projects implemented by IPs in promoting policy reform agenda related to their activity and success to date

5. How well does the FTF program managers here coordinate with donor coordination committee, World Bank, MCC, CADDP, etc. with respect to policy reform promotion and implementation? What has been USAID's role in these efforts?

6. Views on effect of cross-border policy reforms implemented to date on country program FTF outcomes and goals

7. Has there been identification of additional policy or regulatory reforms needed for the success of the FTF program? If so, what is progress in promoting those reforms to date?

FGD with (FTF M&E Manager, Mission Program Officer, and M&E Specialist)

Evaluation question 12. How well has Feed the Future's system and approaches for monitoring, evaluations, and learning (MEL) facilitated requisite levels of accountability and learning? How well have Feed the Future MEL approaches achieved accountability for commitments Feed the Future has made? Has Feed the Future MEL supported improved programming and how?

1. Clarity, utility and application of guidance from BS/SPPM/MEL on M&E approach, FTF Indicator Guide, FTF M&E Guidance Series, Women's Empowerment in Agriculture Index in the Mission FTF Portfolio overall, and in specific projects/activities

2. Confusion among IPs about FTF indicator definitions, data collection and analytical procedures? Are IPs contributing to same indicators using same definitions/approaches to data collection and analysis?

3. Utility of indicators for measuring effectiveness of strategies based on causal pathways and outputs, sub-IRs, IRs, objectives from the FTF RF -what's missing? What isn't working

4. How well is this set of indicators promoting results-based monitoring and accountability to achieve FTF objectives and goals? Does the FTF M&E system promote achievement of outcomes and goals in Mission FTF activities and projects

5. Accessibility to, and utility and use of FTF BFS supported research and learning products, actionable lessons learned to Mission FTF program?

6. Use of data in Mission FTF portfolio reviews, and extent of feeding back performance to date on key indicators to improve activity/project performance.

c. Evaluation Work Plan Schedule

Month/ Activity #	Actions	Deliverable	Participating Team Members	Action Begin: Month/Date	Action Completed: Month/Date	Key Assumptions and Explanatory Notes
February	**Work Plan Submitted, Initial Literature Review Completed and Evaluation Design Begun in February**					
1.	**Draft Work Plan developed and submitted for review**		All team members	**Feb 2**	Feb 12 to Dexis PMU for review Feb 15 to USAID	
1.cont.	**Work Plan finalized based on USAID feedback**	Deliverable 2	Pat	Once comments received	Feb 24	
2.	**Document/Data Review conducted:** Review of scope/type of data sources/documents we have for pertinence for each evaluation question; Read documents, focusing initially on key background documents		All team members	Jan 29	Feb 29	
3.	**Draft of overall evaluation design developed:** • Completed Evaluation Matrix to answer each question as related to 19 focus countries, in-depth evaluation of 4-5	Deliverable 3	Pat, Allyson, Bill, Patricia, Charu and TBD senior evaluation specialist	Feb 15	March 9 to Dexis PMU for review March 10 to USAID	

Month/ Activity #	Actions	Deliverable	Participating Team Members	Action Begin: Month/Date	Action Completed: Month/Date	Key Assumptions and Explanatory Notes
	selected countries, regional programs and Aligned countries, BFS programs • Suggestions for selection of countries for field work based on BFS criteria • Narrative for evaluation design and for plan to analyze data • A coding system to apply to data collection instruments and to document reviews and databases • A comprehensive list of key stakeholders to be interviewed in Washington and in the field with types of questions to be included in KIIs and samples • A suggested list of key stakeholders to include in on-line surveys with types of questions and samples					

Month/ Activity #	Actions	Deliverable	Participating Team Members	Action Begin: Month/Date	Action Completed: Month/Date	Key Assumptions and Explanatory Notes
	• An outline for the evaluation report based on USAID requirements					
4.	**Work with client to:** • **finalize countries** for field work, • **select a subset** of Aligned Countries for in-depth assessment, and • **finalize list of stakeholders** to be interviewed in USAID, other USG participant agencies, and from other organizations as identified (e.g., IPs)		Pat, Natasha, TBD	Feb 15	March 11	End date heavily dependent on responsiveness of FTF core and aligned countries
5.	**Meetings with COR, BFS and SPPM**		Evaluation Team Members	Feb 23	Feb 25	Week of Feb 22 – TBD
March	**Evaluation Design completed in March, Scheduling for DC-based Interviews and In-Country Assessments, Databases Development, Analysis Begins in March**					
6.	Coding system will be applied to all data collection instruments and data sources used for questions will be similarly coded	Deliverable 3	Pat, Allyson, Bill, Patricia TBD senior evaluation specialist	March 6	March 20 to Dexis March 21 to client	These data collection instruments will be altered/questions added once the quantitative

Month/ Activity #	Actions	Deliverable	Participating Team Members	Action Begin: Month/Date	Action Completed: Month/Date	Key Assumptions and Explanatory Notes
	Draft data collection instruments and protocols designed for on-line surveys for 1)19 focus countries, 2) regional country programs, and 3) aligned country programs based on structured review of pertinent data sources and documents Draft data collection instruments and protocols designed for KIIs in Washington, DC and in selected focus countries (list below is incomplete but provides examples) • BFS coordinator and other key managers • SPPM managers • GHFS Coordinator • FTF Country Coordinators • FTF POCs in USG participating agencies in Washington • Managers of the five BFS managed programs					analysis of FTFMS data has been completed. The results of this analysis should yield additional questions to include when interviewing key informants. Changes to all data collection instruments will be thoroughly documented with date and rationale

Month/ Activity #	Actions	Deliverable	Participating Team Members	Action Begin: Month/Date	Action Completed: Month/Date	Key Assumptions and Explanatory Notes
	• In-country managers of FTF programs in aligned core and aligned countries and managers of regional programs (including USAID, and "whole of government" partners in country such as USDA reps, State, etc.) • Government partner officials in core and aligned countries • FTF partners in regional ag research/policy institutes (such as ECOWAS, etc.)					
7.	**Quantitative database developed:** FTF indicator data cleaned, coded and analyzed		TBD senior evaluation specialist	March 7	March 25	FTF data may need cleaning before it can be used for analysis.
8.	**Qualitative database developed**		TBD senior evaluation specialist and Dexis PMU	TBD		
	Presentation of Evaluation Design to External Oversight Committee			TBD		

Month/ Activity #	Actions	Deliverable	Participating Team Members	Action Begin: Month/Date	Action Completed: Month/Date	Key Assumptions and Explanatory Notes
9.	**Final Evaluation Design and Report Outline**: Completed based on feedback from USAID		Pat, Allyson, Patricia, Bill, TBD senior evaluation specialist	March 24	March 31 to Dexis PMU for review April 1 to USAID	Date assumes receipt of USAID comments two weeks following submission on March 10
10.	**Quantitative database populated** with USAID budget allocation data for focus countries where field assessments will be conducted along with FTF Core Investment, Foundational Investment, and Complimentary Investment Data; etc.		TBD	March 28	April 8	These additional data sets will not be included in the data base for regional and aligned country programs or for other focus countries. Length of time to populate data base with this information on countries selected for field work depends on access to these data sets and final decisions on which of these

Month/ Activity #	Actions	Deliverable	Participating Team Members	Action Begin: Month/Date	Action Completed: Month/Date	Key Assumptions and Explanatory Notes
						data sets should be included
11.	**Scheduling in depth Assessment 4-5 FTF focus countries:** scheduling and logistical arrangements for field evaluation countries – Dates/Flights/Clearance/Hotels /Interview Scheduling and Meetings		Dexis PMU	March 14	March 31	Dates depend on responsiveness of selected Missions
12.	**Schedule interviews in Washington, DC** with BFS and SPPM staff, GHFS Coordinator, and stakeholders in USAID and other USG participating agencies (based on list for interviews to be conducted in Washington and by telephone/Skype)		Allyson, Dexis	March 21	March 31	Dates depend on responsiveness of those contacted for interviews
April	**Evaluation Design and Data Collection Instruments Finalized, data collection and analysis begins including field work in selected countries in April**					
13.	**Finalize all data collection instruments and protocols** based on USAID comments		Pat, Allyson, Bill, Patricia, TBD	April 5	April 12 to Dexis PMU April 13 to USAID	Date assumes receipt of USAID comments two weeks following

Month/ Activity #	Actions	Deliverable	Participating Team Members	Action Begin: Month/Date	Action Completed: Month/Date	Key Assumptions and Explanatory Notes
						submission on March 22
14.	**All on-line surveys transmitted**		Charu and Dexis PMU	April 14		Transmittal date depends on USAID clearance
15.	**Assess performance of 19 Focus countries** – combining March assessment of FTF performance data and other pertinent quantitative data sets		TBD	April 10	May 6	Dates assume USAID clearance on evaluation design
16.	**Finalize logistical arrangements for field** evaluation countries, finalize calendar and meetings for in-country field work		Dexis PMU with input from team	April 4	April 11	
17.	**Field Work:** Team members prepare for field work, are deployed, complete assessments and provide initial debriefs pre-departure. Interview recordings are uploaded each day and sent for transcription. Interview transcripts are downloaded into qualitative		Pat, Bill, Patricia, Charu	April 8 preparation for field work followed by deployment	May 27	Dates are estimates and depend on approval of data collection instruments designed for field work and scheduling. All field work should

Month/ Activity #	Actions	Deliverable	Participating Team Members	Action Begin: Month/Date	Action Completed: Month/Date	Key Assumptions and Explanatory Notes
	database for later qualitative analysis					be completed NLT May 27
18.	**Assess Focus, Regional and Aligned Programs:** Collect and analyze data from on-line surveys and other pertinent data sources		TBD senior evaluation specialist	April 18	May 13	Completion date assumes receipt of online survey data
19.	**Conduct Interviews in Washington, DC and by telephone/Skype: BFS programs and BFS FTF Management:** Conduct interviews with BFS, SPPM. GHFS Coordinator and other key stakeholders in USAID and participating USG agencies Interview recordings are uploaded each day and sent for transcription. Interview transcripts are downloaded qualitative analysis		Allyson, TBD	April 15	May 13	Dates depend on scheduling
May	**All data collection ends and analysis continues in May**					
20.	**Conduct analysis of all data sources for each evaluation question:** quantitative data		Pat, Allyson, Bill, Patricia, TBD senior	May 2	June 10	Analysis conducted on rolling basis as data sets are

Month/ Activity #	Actions	Deliverable	Participating Team Members	Action Begin: Month/Date	Action Completed: Month/Date	Key Assumptions and Explanatory Notes
	per question, qualitative data per question		evaluation specialist			available from each source
June	Debriefing, Analysis ends and Writing Begins in June					
21.	Conduct debrief of fieldwork and all other data collection activities for BFS, IEP, EOC, etc.	Deliverable 6	Evaluation Team	June 6		Date depends on USAID scheduling
22.	Data analysis and writing conducted per evaluation question – drawing together analysis from quantitative and qualitative data sets		Responsibility per question TBD	June 13	June 24	
23.	Draft evaluation report: Draft report written and edited including illustrations, annex and submitted to Dexis	Deliverable 7	Pat , Laurie, TBD senior evaluation specialist	June 20	July 6 submit to Dexis PMU for review	Weeks 2 and 3 in June
	Present initial findings and information for draft report to EOC					Should be presented to EOC before draft is finalized
July	Review of Evaluation Report, Finalization of Draft and Submission to Client in July					
23. continue d	Draft report finalized based on Dexis review, submitted to USAID	Deliverable 7	Pat and Laurie	July 11	July 15 Submit to USAID for review	
August	Finalization of Evaluation Report and Presentation in August – Activity Six Completed					

Month/ Activity #	Actions	Deliverable	Participating Team Members	Action Begin: Month/Date	Action Completed: Month/Date	Key Assumptions and Explanatory Notes
24.	**Draft Report revised and finalized** based on IEP and EOC Comments; submitted to Dexis	Deliverable 8	Pat, Laurie and other team members as needed	August 8	August 19 submit to Dexis PMU for review	Dates depend on receipt of USAID comments
25. continue d	**Final evaluation report completed** based on Dexis review and submitted to USAID	Deliverable 8	Pat, Laurie	August 23	August 25 submit to USAID	
26.	**Presentation of evaluation at USAID**	Deliverable 9	Evaluation Team			TBD based on USAID scheduling
	Presentation of evaluation final report to EOC		Evaluation Team			
Decembe r	**Posting of Final Report and Data Sets in December**					
27.	**Final report and data sets posted**	Deliverable 10	Dexis			TBD based on USAID final acceptance of evaluation report.

a. Online Survey: Focus Countries

INTRODUCTION

Thank you for taking out valuable time to respond to this survey. This survey was sent to Mission Feed the Future Team Lead/Coordinators, and each mission can provide two responses (respondents) for the survey.

To minimize the time it takes to respond to this survey, the majority of the questions are designed as multiple choices for you to check off your responses. At the same time, we strongly encourage you to provide explanations to your answers in the comment box following every question as your ideas and feedback are important in informing modifications or adjustment to Feed the Future initiative.

1. Please select which mission you work with.

Monitoring, Evaluation and Learning Questions

The Feed the Future monitoring, evaluation and learning (MEL) approach is based on the Feed the Future Results Framework, which establishes the goals and objectives of the initiative; a performance monitoring process and standard performance indicators to track progress toward desired results; local human and institutional capacity-building investment to improve the quality and frequency of data collection and use; performance evaluations and impact evaluations to examine how programs are working and to determine the measurable effects of Feed the Future investments; and knowledge-sharing activities to foster learning and use of M&E findings.

2. How helpful have the Feed the Future Guide and M&E Guidance documents, support from BFS personnel, and BFS-managed M&E implementing mechanisms been in ***clarifying the Feed the Future MEL approach and how to apply it?***

Please check the response that applies to each resource listed in the left hand column of the table.

Resources	0 Not aware of this resource	1 Have not consulted/ Have not attended	2 Not helpful At all	3 Not very helpful	4 Somewhat helpful	5 Helpful	6 Very helpful
Feed the Future Guide 2010							
Results Framework document							
Vol. 1: M&E Under Feed the Future: M&E Approach							
Feed the Future Indicator Handbook							
Frequently Asked Questions: Feed the Future M&E Approach							
Support from BFS personnel							
Support from BFS-managed MEL mechanisms							
Other: Please write in							
Other: Please write in							

Comments:

3. How helpful have Feed the Future documents from the M&E Guidance Series, other guidance documents, support from BFS personnel and support from BFS MEL implementing mechanisms been in ***clarifying how to collect and analyze data*** for Feed the Future indicators?

Please check the response that applies to each resource listed in the left hand column in the table below.

Resources	0 Not aware of this	1 Have not used	2 Not helpful At all	3 Not very helpful	4 Somewhat helpful	5 Helpful	6 Very helpful
Feed the Future Indicator Handbook							
Feed the Future Agricultural Indicators Guide							
M&E Guidance Series Vol. 5: Measuring Local Capacity Development							
M&E Guidance Series Vol. 6: Measuring the Gender Impact of Feed the Future							
M&E Guidance Series Vol. 7: Measuring Natural Resources Management and Climate Change Resiliency							
M&E Guidance Series Vol. 8: Population Based Survey Instrument for Feed the Future Zone of Influence Indicators							
M&E Guidance Series Vol. 9.1: Target Setting for Reducing the Prevalence of Poverty							
M&E Guidance Series Vol. 11: Guidance on the Interim Assessment of the Feed the Future ZOI Population Level Indicators							
Guide for applying Women's Empowerment							

Resources	0 Not aware of this	1 Have not used	2 Not helpful At all	3 Not very helpful	4 Somewhat helpful	5 Helpful	6 Very helpful
in Agriculture Index (WEAI)							
Feed the Future Gender Integration Framework							
BFS-led training and workshops							
Support from BFS MEL implementing mechanisms							
Other: Please write in							
Other: Please write in							

Comments:

4. How helpful is the Feed the Future standard indicator framework and FTFMS reporting in promoting achievements and accountability for Feed the Future commitments?

   1 Not helpful at all
   2 Not very helpful
   3 Somewhat helpful
   4 Helpful
   5 Very helpful
   6 Do not know

Comments:

5. How helpful is the population-based survey approach for monitoring impacts and outcomes in promoting achievements and accountability for Feed the Future commitments?

1 Not helpful at all
2 Not very helpful
3 Somewhat helpful
4 Helpful
5 Very helpful
6 Do not know

Comments:

6. How helpful is the development and application of the Feed the Future Learning Agenda in promoting achievements and accountability for Feed the Future commitments?

1 Not helpful at all
2 Not very helpful
3 Somewhat helpful
4 Helpful
5 Very helpful
6 Do not know

Comments:

7. How well do the indicators under the Feed the Future standard indicator framework/handbook enable your mission to track key objectives related to your program?

Please check all that apply.

1	The standard indicator framework provides useful indicators to track every key objective of our program.	
2	The standard indicator framework provides useful indicators to track most of the key objective of our program.	
3	The standard indicator framework ***does not*** provide useful indicators to track most of the key objective of our program.	

4	The standard indicator framework provides too many indicators.	
5	There are too many **required** indicators under the standard indicator framework.	
6	Most of the indicators included in the standard indicator framework are irrelevant to the objectives of our Feed the Future program.	
7	Many of the indicators included in the standard indicator framework are too difficult to measure or track.	

Comments:

8. How accurately does the Feed the Future Results Framework (RF) reflect the development hypotheses of your mission's program and the causal pathways that lead from Feed the Future programmatic outcomes to the goals of reducing poverty and stunting?

Please check all that apply.

1	The RF reflects all causal relationships in the development hypotheses underlying our Feed the Future program.	
2	The RF reflects most of the causal relationships of the development hypotheses of our program, but not all. Some relevant causal links are not represented.	
3	The RF does not reflect many aspects of the development hypotheses underlying our Feed the Future program. Many relevant causal links are missing.	
4	The RF includes causal relationships that are not relevant to the food security situation in the country where I work.	
5	Critical causal relationships related to agricultural growth are missing from the RF.	
6	Critical causal relationships related to nutrition are missing from the RF.	

Comments:

Zone of Influence Questions

9. How effective is focusing Feed the Future programs in a specific Zone of Influence (ZOI) in achieving targeted goals and objectives?

Please check all that apply.

1	Focusing programs in a ZOI enabled our programs to meet Feed the Future goals and/or objectives.	
2	Focusing programs in a ZOI limited our ability to meet goals and/or objectives.	
3	Having a ZOI improved our ability to monitor progress.	
4	Having a ZOI **did not improve** our ability to monitor progress.	
5	Focusing programs in a ZOI effectively focused our resources.	
6	Focusing programs in ZOI caused us to miss opportunities to meet goals and/or objectives.	
7	More geographic flexibility is needed in program design to meet Feed the Future goals.	

Comments:

10. To what extent have **nutritional and agricultural interventions** been scaled up across the Zone of Influence (ZOI)?

Please check your responses for nutritional and agricultural interventions.	Nutritional	Agricultural
0 = not at all		
1 = Implementing partners (IP) are currently in the process of scaling up to meet their targets within the ZOI		

Please check your responses for nutritional and agricultural interventions.	Nutritional	Agricultural
2 = IPs have scaled up across the ZOI and have met their targets for coverage of households		
3 = IPs are reaching more households than originally targeted within the ZOI		
4 = IPs have now covered all applicable households in the ZOI.		
5 = Other. Please write in		

Comments:

11. Is the proportion of households being reached by Feed the Future activities in the ZOI sufficient to plausibly achieve the five-year targets for reducing the prevalence of poverty and stunting by 2017?

Please check your response for each indicator.	Prevalence of Poverty	Prevalence of Stunting
0 = No		
1 = Not able to tell at this time		
2 = Will be close to the target		
3 = Yes, or will exceed the target		

Comments:

Value Chain Questions

12. How effective is the value chain approach employed by Feed the Future (targeting a limited number of value chain commodities and working through various links in the value chain) in achieving targeted goals and objectives?

Please check all that apply.

1	The value chain approach limited our ability to meet goals and/or objectives.	
2	The value chain approach effectively focused our resources.	
3	The value chain approach enabled our programs to meet goals and/or objectives.	
4	Focus on a value chain approach caused us to miss opportunities to meet our goals and/or objectives.	
5	The value chain approach could be effective, but our selection of specific value chains may have limited our ability to meet goals and/or objectives.	
6	More flexibility is needed in program design to meet Feed the Future goals.	

Comments:

13. Are your Implementing Partners integrating nutrition interventions in value chain activities they are implementing?

    0 = no
    1 = some of them are
    2 = yes

If your answer is no, please skip to question 15.

Comments:

14. If your answer is yes, how have you integrated nutrition into Value Chains (VC)?

Please check all that apply.

1	VC selected in part due to nutritional value (includes grains, roots and tubers; legumes and nuts; animal-sourced foods; foods from horticulture. Production must be for domestic market)	
2	VC production work includes some assistance to the production of non-VC crops that are staples of smallholders	
3	Promotion of home self-consumption of surplus production of VC commodity	
4	Water infrastructure investments for VC commodity improve water quality for domestic use.	
6	Improved agricultural inputs, time- and labor-saving technology for women producers	
7	Intercropping of nutrient dense commodities with value chain crop	
8	Nutrition and/or health promotion to value chain actors	
9	Provision of health services to value chain actors	
10	Saving and loans groups to support domestic needs (ex. health care seeking)	
11	Promotion of home gardens or other production for household consumption among value chain actors	
12	Other: please describe	
13	Other: please describe	

Comments:

15. If your answer is yes to Question 12, do you have any evidence to suggest that this integration makes a difference in achieving nutrition objectives? If yes, please describe the evidence in the comment box below.

   0 = yes

   1 = no

   2 = not able to tell at this time

3 = no information to make a comparison

Comments:

16. If your answer was no to Question 12, what strategic approaches has the mission taken to ensure nutrition objectives are met?

Please check all that apply.

1	Co-locating agriculture and nutrition interventions	
2	Locating nutrition interventions in areas with highest rates of undernutrition	
3	Modifying existing activities to incorporate new or strengthened nutrition interventions to respond to Feed the Future objectives, e.g., research and extension building back up the local seed system for basic staples	
4	Ministry of Health and Ministry of Agriculture evolving to work together to ensure nutrition interventions are incorporated into agricultural activities	
5	Other. Please write in	
6	Other. Please write in	

Comments:

Private Sector Questions

17. How many partnerships with private sector entities has the Mission developed to date to support agriculture or nutrition interventions?

Please write in the number.

Agriculture Interventions	Nutrition Interventions

Comments:

18. What have been the specific contributions to date from private sector companies that are involved in the Mission's Feed the Future activities and programs?

	Please check all that apply	
1	agricultural inputs	
2	training to use agricultural inputs	
3	training to ensure consistent quality of agricultural products (plants/animals/dairy)	
4	financing for producers	
5	equipment for producers	
6	Storage	
7	cold storage	
8	post-harvest processing equipment	
9	financing for post-harvest value added	
8	labeling/packaging for domestic sale or export	
9	new markets for products	
10	transportation of products for exporting to markets	
11	improved transportation corridors	
12	buyer for agricultural products from Feed the Future activities	
13	nutritional foods for children five years of age and under	
14	vitamins for children five years of age and under	
15	Other. Please write in.	
16	Other. Please write in.	
17	Other. Please write in.	

Comments:

19. Were government partners involved in negotiation of arrangements for the private sector companies that are currently participating in the Feed the Future initiative as partners?

        0 = No

        1 = Yes

        2 = On a limited basis

Comments:

20. In your opinion, will the government continue to promote private sector investment, marketing and commercial dissemination in agricultural and nutrition programs after the Feed the Future initiative is over?

> 0 = No
> 1 = Uncertain
> 2 = Unlikely
> 3 = On a limited basis
> 4 = Yes

Comments:

Human and Institutional Capacity Development Questions

21. What type of human and institutional capacity development (HICD) interventions has the Mission implemented to date that have **succeeded** in increasing the capacity of your government partners to effectively undertake interventions related to their roles in the partnership in both the agriculture and nutrition sectors?

Please check all that apply in each sector		Agriculture sector	Nutrition sector
0	On-the-job training (OJT)		
1	Mentoring		
2	Workshops		
3	Improving information systems		
4	Training to increase data collection and analytical capabilities (use of information systems)		
5	Improving ICT capabilities		
6	New or replacement equipment		
7	Funding for facility upgrades		
8	Other: Please write in		
9	Other: Please write in		

Comments:

22. Have you had assistance from BFS centrally managed HICD activities to increase staff capacity in any of the partnering ministries at the national, regional or local level?

        0 = Yes

        1 = No

Please skip to question 23 if your answer is no

Comments:

23. If you replied yes, was that assistance well-coordinated with the Mission's **own efforts** to increase capacity?

        1 = Not at all coordinated with Mission identified HICD needs

        2 = Not very well coordinated

        3 = Somewhat

        4 = Coordinated

        5 = Very Well Coordinated

Comments:

Regional Policy Intervention Questions

24. To which objectives in the FTF RF have your policy activities made a significant contribution? Please check all that apply.

Sustainable reductions in poverty	
Sustainable reductions in hunger (stunting)	
Inclusive agricultural sector growth	
Improved nutritional status, especially of women and children	
Improved agricultural productivity	
Expanding markets and trade	
Increased investment in agriculture and nutrition related activities	

Increased employment opportunities in targeted value chain activities	
Increased resilience of vulnerable communities and households	
Improved access to diverse and quality foods	
Improved nutrition-related behaviors	
Improved use of maternal and child health and nutrition services	
No significant contributions to objectives in the FTF Results Framework	

Comments:

25. Is the USAID Regional Mission's program in your area promoting legal and regulatory reforms to increase regional or cross-border trade that will contribute to your Mission's Feed the Future program in the following ways?

Please check your response for each intervention listed below.

	Interventions	No	Yes, In process	Yes, Completed
1	Streamlining customs practices for clearing agricultural goods across borders			
2	Regional harmonization of grades and standards for key staple foods			
3	Reduction of tariffs and fees for moving staple foods across borders			
4	Development of regional MIS to promote timely information on prices, bids and offers for key food staple crops across the region			
5	Development of value chain specific regional associations to facilitate trade, access to finance, advocate for policy changes, etc.			

Interventions		No	Yes, In process	Yes, Completed
6	Interventions to increase women's participation in regional trade			
7	Other: please write in.			
8	Other: please write in			

Comments:

26. Has the successful implementation of regional/trans-border reforms to date made a positive contribution toward progress in meeting the Mission's targets for any of the following Feed the Future indicators in this country?

Please check your response for each of the following Feed the Future indicators.

Feed the Future Indicators		Yes	No	N/A
	Gross margin per hectare, animal or cage of selected product			
2	Value of intra-regional trade in agricultural commodities			
3	Value of exports for targeted agricultural commodities			
4	Value of incremental sales			
5	Number of jobs			
6	Numbers of agricultural and nutritional enabling environment policies completing the following processes/steps of development as a result of USG assistance in each case: analysis; stakeholder consultation/public debate; drafting or revision; approval (legislative or regulatory); full and effective implementation			
7	Other: please write in:			
8	Other: please write in:			
9	No contributions to meeting targets in any Feed the Future indicators the Mission reports on			

Comments:

Learning Questions

27. Have you used Feed the Future learning products in any of the following thematic areas?

Please check your response for each of the thematic areas listed across the top of the table.

Thematic Areas	Improved Agricultural Productivity	Improved Research & Development	Expanded Markets, Value Chains & Increased Investment	Improved Nutrition & Dietary Quality	Improved Gender Integration & Women's Empowerment	Improved Resilience of Vulnerable Populations
0 – I am not aware of any of learning products related to this theme						
1 – I am aware of learning products related to this theme but have not examined them						
2 – I have looked at learning products from this theme but there are no findings that can be applied to our program						
3 – We are discussing some of the actionable lessons learned among members of our Feed the Future team and/or partners						
4- We have applied some of the actionable lessons learned to our Feed the Future activities but it is too early to determine the benefit to support Feed the Future program outcomes and goals.						
5. We have attempted to apply some of the actionable lessons learned to our Feed the Future activities but found implementation was not practical or cost-efficient for our country program						
6. We have applied some of the actionable lessons learned to our activities and there is some indication that it will prove						

Thematic Areas	Improved Agricultural Productivity	Improved Research & Development	Expanded Markets, Value Chains & Increased Investment	Improved Nutrition & Dietary Quality	Improved Gender Integration & Women's Empowerment	Improved Resilience of Vulnerable Populations
beneficial to the Feed the Future program						

Comments:

28. In what ways does your Mission Feed the Future team use Agrilinks?

Please check all that apply.

1	To learn about recent innovations that may be useful/applicable to our program	
2	To learn about upcoming training opportunities and webinars	
3	To access resources useful for the design of new Feed the Future activities	
4	To participate in groups (e.g. Agriculture and Nutrition Global Learning and Evidence Exchange, Extension and Advisory Services Group, etc.)	
5	To share experiences and lessons learned in blogs	
6	To learn about upcoming events (e.g. Agriculture Sector Council Seminars)	
7	Our team does not use Agrilinks.	
8	Other: Please write in.	

Comments:

29. What resources has the Mission Feed the Future team found to be valuable that were sourced from the Agrilinks website?

Please check all that apply.

1	Links to webinars	
2	Blogs	
3	Groups	
4	Notice of upcoming events such as Ag Sector Council Seminars	
5	Reports on recent research findings	

6	Articles on how to implement cross-cutting activities such as climate smart agriculture, nutrition sensitive agriculture, gender, etc.	
7	Recent evaluations related to Feed the Future topics	
8	None.	
9	Other: Please write in	
10	Other: Please write in	

Comments:

Research Questions

The Feed the Future Research Strategy is organized around seven key challenge (program) areas related to sustainably transforming agricultural production systems, ensuring access to nutritious and safe foods, creating enabling and supportive policies, and addressing the emerging challenges of climate change and natural resources scarcity. Feed the Future research may be funded through a variety of mechanisms including Innovation Labs with U.S. Universities, cooperative agreements with private companies, and various CGIAR grants –such as Africa RISING and Bio-safety programs.

30. How useful are the research products, technical assistance and support offered in each program area through the Feed the Future centrally-managed research mechanisms in contributing to agriculture and nutrition outcomes in this country?

Please check responses for each program area listed in the left hand column.

Research Program areas	Not aware of research products, findings, assistance or support in this program area	Have not drawn on resources related to this program area	Not relevant to our Feed the Future portfolio	Not useful at all	Somewhat useful	Useful	Very Useful	IPs have applied research findings/products to Feed the Future activities
Climate-Resilient Cereals (i.e. CGIAR maize, wheat, and rice programs)								

Research Program areas	Not aware of research products, findings, assistance or support in this program area	Have not drawn on resources related to this program area	Not relevant to our Feed the Future portfolio	Not useful at all	Somewhat useful	Useful	Very Useful	IPs have applied research findings/products to Feed the Future activities
Legume Productivity (i.e. Peanut and Mycotoxin Innovation Lab and Legume Innovation Lab)								
Advanced Approaches to Combat Pests and Diseases (i.e. BT Cowpea and BT Eggplant)								
Research on Nutritious and Safe Foods (i.e. Nutrition and Horticulture Innovation Labs)								
Markets and Policy Research (i.e AMA-BASIS Innovation Lab)								
Sustainable Intensification (i.e. Africa RISING)								
Human and Institutional Capacity Development (i.e. BHEARD)								

Comments:

31. For the technologies (e.g. crop varieties) and knowledge disseminated in Feed the Future country programs, what is the source of these technologies/knowledge?

Please check all that apply

1	U.S. University partnerships with National Agriculture Research Systems	
2	CGIAR centers	
3	local private companies	
4	local universities	
5	Other: please specify	
6	Other: please specify	
7	Other please specify	

Comments:

32. Are there any Feed the Future sponsored research trials going on in this country now?

    0   = no
    1   = yes
    2   = completed

Comments:

33. If you replied "yes" or "completed" to question 33, please provide a brief description of what is or has been trialed and the outcome of that trial.

Comments:

34. Are any research products that were trialed (technologies, seeds, etc.) currently being scaled up for use across the Zone of Influence at the current time?
    0   = no, and don't plan to
    1   = no, but plan to
    2   = yes
    3   = completed

Comments:

35. If you replied "yes" or "completed" to question 36, please provide a brief description of what is or has been scaled up and outcomes seen to date.

Comments:

36. To what extent do you feel that the various research projects in this country are integrated with the overall Feed the Future program?

> 1 – Not at all
> 2 - Not very well
> 3 – Somewhat
> 4 – Well integrated
> 5 – Very well integrated

Comments:

37. To what extent do you feel that the various research projects in this country complement each other or build synergies?

> 1 – Not at all
> 2 - Not very well
> 3 – Somewhat
> 4 – Complementary
> 5 – Very complimentary

Comments:

Centrally-managed Mechanisms

Centrally-managed mechanisms are intended to complement Mission programs and engagement by focusing on regional or global dimensions that improve the efficiency and effectiveness of mission programs. To improve the complementarity of USAID investment, mission vs central program roles must be balanced.

38. From your experience, how well have centrally-managed mechanisms contributed to your mission's efforts to achieve your goals and objectives?

Please check all that apply.

1	Central mechanisms **have not been** well-coordinated with the Mission.	
2	Central mechanisms have been well-coordinated with the Mission.	
3	Central mechanisms provide access to important activities for our portfolio.	
4	Central mechanisms reduce procurement burden on Missions.	
5	Central mechanisms **have not fit** the Mission's programmatic needs.	
6	Central mechanisms **have not contributed** to achieving our Feed the Future goals and objectives.	
7	We have not accessed central mechanisms.	

Comments:

Thank you very much for taking the time to respond to the questions in this survey.

INTRODUCTION

Thank you for taking out valuable time to respond to this survey. It is designed to obtain data for the Global Performance Evaluation of the Feed the Future initiative. This survey was sent to Mission Feed the Future Team Lead/Coordinators, and each mission can provide two responses (respondents) for the survey.

To minimize the time it takes to respond to this survey, the majority of the questions are designed as multiple choices for you to check off your responses. At the same time, we strongly encourage you to provide explanations to your answers in the comment box following every question as your ideas and feedback are important in informing modifications or adjustment to Feed the Future initiative.

1. Please select which Mission you work with.

Monitoring, Evaluation and Learning Questions

The Feed the Future monitoring, evaluation and learning (MEL) approach is based on the Feed the Future Results Framework, which establishes the goals and objectives of the initiative; a performance monitoring process and standard performance indicators to track progress toward desired results; local human and institutional capacity-building investment to improve the quality and frequency of data collection and use; performance evaluations and impact evaluations to examine how programs are working and to determine the measurable effects of Feed the Future investments; and knowledge-sharing activities to foster learning and use of M&E findings.

2. How helpful have the Feed the Future Guide and M&E Guidance documents, support from BFS personnel, and BFS-managed M&E implementing mechanisms been in *clarifying the Feed the Future MEL approach and how to apply it?*

Please check the response that applies to each resource listed in the left hand column of the table.

Resources	0 Not aware of this resource	1 Have not consulted/ Have not attended	2 Not helpful At all	3 Not very helpful	4 Somewhat helpful	5 Helpful	6 Very helpful
Feed the Future Guide 2010							
Results Framework document							
Vol. 1: M&E Under Feed the Future: MEL Approach							
Feed the Future Indicator Handbook							
Frequently Asked Questions: Feed the Future MEL Approach							
Support from BFS personnel							
Support from BFS-managed MEL mechanisms							
Other: Please write in							
Other: Please write in							
Other: Please write in							

Comments:

3. How helpful have Feed the Future documents from the M&E Guidance Series, other guidance documents, support from BFS personnel and support from BFS MEL implementing mechanisms been in **clarifying how to collect and analyze data** for Feed the Future indicators?

Please check the response that applies to each resource listed in the left hand column in the table below.

Resources	0 Not aware of this	1 Not applicable	2 Have not used	3 Not helpful At all	4 Not very helpful	5 Somewhat helpful	6 Helpful	7 Very helpful
Feed the Future Indicator Handbook								
Feed the Future Agricultural Indicators Guide								
M&E Guidance Series Vol. 5: Measuring Local Capacity Development								
M&E Guidance Series Vol. 6: Measuring the Gender Impact of Feed the Future								
M&E Guidance Series Vol. 7: Measuring Natural Resources Management and Climate Change Resiliency								
M&E Guidance Series Vol. 9.1: Target Setting for Reducing the Prevalence of Poverty								
Guide for applying Women's Empowerment in Agriculture Index (WEAI)								
Feed the Future Gender Integration Framework								
BFS led training and workshops								
Support from BFS MEL implementing mechanisms								
Other: Please write in								
Other: Please write in								

Comments:

4. How helpful is the Feed the Future standard indicator framework and FTFMS reporting in promoting achievements and accountability for Feed the Future commitments?

   7   Not helpful at all
   8   Not very helpful
   9   Somewhat helpful
   10 Helpful
   11 Very helpful
   12 Do not know

Comments:

5. How helpful is the development and application of the Feed the Future Learning Agenda in promoting achievements and accountability for Feed the Future commitments?

   7   Not helpful at all
   8   Not very helpful
   9   Somewhat helpful
   10 Helpful
   11 Very helpful
   12 Do not know

Comments:

6. How well do the indicators under the Feed the Future standard indicator framework/handbook enable your mission to track key objectives related to your program?

Please check all that apply.

1	The standard indicator framework provides useful indicators to track every key objective of our program.	

2	The standard indicator framework provides useful indicators to track most of the key objective of our program.	
3	The standard indicator framework **does not** provide useful indicators to track most of the key objective of our program.	
4	The standard indicator framework provides too many indicators.	
5	There are too many **required** indicators under the standard indicator framework.	
6	Most of the indicators included in the standard indicator framework are irrelevant to the objectives of our Feed the Future program.	
7	Many of the indicators included in the standard indicator framework are too difficult to measure or track.	

Comments:

7. How accurately does the Feed the Future Results Framework (RF) reflect the development hypotheses of your mission's program and the causal pathways that lead from Feed the Future programmatic outcomes to the goals of reducing poverty and stunting?

Please check all that apply.

1	The RF reflects all causal relationships in the development hypotheses underlying our Feed the Future program.	
2	The RF reflects most of the causal relationships of the development hypotheses of our program, but not all. Some relevant causal links are not represented.	
3	The RF does not reflect many aspects of the development hypotheses underlying our Feed the Future program. Many relevant causal links are missing.	
4	The RF includes causal relationships that are not relevant to the food security situation in the country where I work.	
5	Critical causal relationships related to agricultural growth are missing from the RF.	
6	Critical causal relationships related to nutrition are missing from the RF.	

Comments:

Value Chain Questions (if applicable)

8. How effective is the value chain approach employed by Feed the Future (targeting a limited number of value chain commodities and working through various links in the value chain) in achieving targeted goals and objectives?

Please check all that apply.

1	The value chain approach limited our ability to meet goals and/or objectives.	
2	The value chain approach effectively focused our resources.	
3	The value chain approach enabled our programs to meet goals and/or objectives.	
4	Focus on a value chain approach caused us to miss opportunities to meet our goals and/or objectives.	
5	The value chain approach could be effective, but our selection of specific value chains may have limited our ability to meet goals and/or objectives.	
6	More flexibility is needed in program design to meet Feed the Future goals.	

Comments:

9. Are your Implementing Partners integrating nutrition interventions in value chain activities they are implementing?

0 = no
1 = some of them are
2 = yes

If your answer is no, please skip to question 11.

Comments:

10. If your answer is yes, how have you integrated nutrition into Value Chains (VC)?

Please check all that apply.

1	VC selected in part due to nutritional value (includes grains, roots and tubers; legumes and nuts; animal-sourced foods; foods from horticulture. Production must be for domestic market)	

2	VC production work includes some assistance to the production of non-VC crops that are staples of smallholders	
3	Promotion of home self-consumption of surplus production of VC commodity	
4	Water infrastructure investments for VC commodity improve water quality for domestic use.	
5	Improved agricultural inputs, time- and labor-saving technology for women producers	
6	Intercropping of nutrient dense commodities with value chain crop	
7	Nutrition and/or health promotion to value chain actors	
8	Provision of health services to value chain actors	
9	Saving and loans groups to support domestic needs (ex. health care seeking)	
10	Promotion of home gardens or other production for household consumption among value chain actors	
11	Other: please describe	
12	Other: please describe	

Comments:

11. If your answer is yes to Question 8, do you have any evidence to suggest that this integration makes a difference in achieving nutrition objectives? If yes, please describe the evidence in the comment box below.

    0 = yes

    1 = no

    2 = not able to tell at this time

    3 = no information to make a comparison

Comments:

12. If your answer was no to Question 8, what strategic approaches has the mission taken to ensure nutrition objectives are met?

Please check all that apply.

1	Co-locating agriculture and nutrition interventions	
2	Locating nutrition interventions in areas with highest rates of undernutrition	
3	Modifying existing activities to incorporate new or strengthened nutrition interventions to respond to Feed the Future objectives, e.g., research and extension building back up the local seed system for basic staples	
4	Ministry of Health and Ministry of Agriculture evolving to work together to ensure nutrition interventions are incorporated into agricultural activities	
5	Other. Please write in	
6	Other. Please write in	

Comments:

Private Sector Questions

13. How many partnerships with private sector entities has the Mission developed to date to support agriculture or nutrition interventions?

   Please write in the number.

Agriculture Interventions	Nutrition Interventions

Comments:

14. What have been the specific contributions to date from private sector companies that are involved in the Mission's Feed the Future activities and programs?

Please check all that apply	
1	agricultural inputs	

2	training to use agricultural inputs	
3	training to ensure consistent quality of agricultural products (plants/animals/dairy)	
4	financing for producers	
5	equipment for producers	
6	Storage	
7	cold storage	
8	post-harvest processing equipment	
9	financing for post-harvest value added	
8	labeling/packaging for domestic sale or export	
9	new markets for products	
10	transportation of products for exporting to markets	
11	improved transportation corridors	
12	buyer for agricultural products from Feed the Future activities	
13	nutritional foods for children five years of age and under	
14	vitamins for children five years of age and under	
15	Other. Please write in.	
16	Other. Please write in.	
17	Other. Please write in.	

Comments:

Capacity Development Questions

15. What type of human and institutional capacity development (HICD) interventions have you implemented to date that have **succeeded** in increasing the capacity of your government partners to effectively undertake interventions related to their roles in the partnership in both the agriculture and nutrition sectors?

Please check all that apply		**Agriculture sector**	**Nutrition sector**
0	On-the-job training (OJT)		
1	Mentoring		

Please check all that apply		Agriculture sector	Nutrition sector
2	Workshops:		
3	Improving information systems		
	Training to increase data collection and analytical capabilities (use of information systems)		
4	Improving ICT capabilities		
5	New or replacement equipment		
6	Funding for facility upgrades		
7	Other: Please write in		
8	Other: Please write in		

Comments:

16. Have you had assistance from BFS centrally managed HICD activities to increase staff capacity in any of the partnering institutions/organizations (government/non-government) you work with at the national or local level?

> 0 = No
> 1 = Yes
> 2 = Not applicable

Please skip to question 17 if your answer is no

Comments:

17. If you replied yes, was that assistance well-coordinated with the mission's ***own efforts*** to increase capacity?

> 1 = Not at all coordinated with Mission identified HICD needs
> 2 = Not very well coordinated
> 3 = Somewhat
> 4 = Coordinated
> 5 = Very Well Coordinated

Comments:

Learning Questions

18. Have you used Feed the Future learning products in any of the following thematic areas?

Please check your response for each of the thematic areas listed across the top of the table.

Thematic areas	Improved Agricultural Productivity	Improved Research & Development	Expanded Markets, Value Chains & Increased Investment	Improved Nutrition & Dietary Quality	Improved Gender Integration & Women's Empowerment	Improved Resilience of Vulnerable Populations
0 – I am not aware of any of learning products related to this theme						
1 – I am aware of learning products related to this theme but have not examined them						
2 – I have looked at learning products from this theme but there are no findings that can be applied to our program						
3 – We are discussing some of the actionable lessons learned among members of our team and/or partners						
4- We have applied some of the actionable lessons learned to our Feed						

Thematic areas	Improved Agricultural Productivity	Improved Research & Development	Expanded Markets, Value Chains & Increased Investment	Improved Nutrition & Dietary Quality	Improved Gender Integration & Women's Empowerment	Improved Resilience of Vulnerable Populations
the Future activities but it is too early to determine the benefit to support Feed the Future program outcomes and goals.						
5. We have attempted to apply some of the actionable lessons learned to our activities but found implementation was not practical or cost-efficient for our country program.						
6. We have applied some of the actionable lessons learned to our activities and there is some indication that it will prove beneficial to the Feed the Future program						

Comments:

19. In what ways does your Mission use Agrilinks?

Please check all that apply.

1	To learn about recent innovations that may be useful/applicable to our program	

2	To learn about upcoming training opportunities and webinars	
3	To access resources useful for the design of new Feed the Future activities	
4	To participate in groups (e.g. Agriculture and Nutrition Global Learning and Evidence Exchange, Extension and Advisory Services Group, etc.)	
5	To share experiences and lessons learned in blogs	
6	To learn about upcoming events (e.g. Agriculture Sector Council Seminars)	
7	Do not use Agrilinks.	
8	Other: Please write in.	

Comments:

20. What resources has the Mission found to be valuable that were sourced from the Agrilinks website?

Please check all that apply.

1	Links to webinars	
2	Blogs	
3	Groups	
4	Notice of upcoming events such as Ag Sector Council Seminars	
5	Reports on recent research findings	
6	Articles on how to implement cross-cutting activities such as climate smart agriculture, nutrition sensitive agriculture, gender, etc.	
7	Recent evaluations related to Feed the Future topics	
8	None.	
9	Other: Please write in	
10	Other: Please write in	

Comments:

Research Questions

The Feed the Future Research Strategy is organized around seven key challenge (program) areas related to sustainably transforming agricultural production systems, ensuring access to nutritious and safe foods, creating enabling and supportive policies, and addressing the emerging challenges of climate change and natural resources scarcity. Feed the Future research may be funded through a variety of mechanisms including Innovation Labs with U.S. Universities, cooperative agreements with private companies, and various CGIAR grants –such as Africa RISING and Bio-safety programs.

21. How useful are the research products, technical assistance and support offered in each program area through the Feed the Future centrally-managed research mechanisms in contributing to agriculture and nutrition outcomes in this country?

Please check responses for each program area listed in the left hand column.

Research Program areas	Not aware of research products, findings, assistance or support in this program area	Have not drawn on resources related to this program area	Not relevant to our portfolio	Not useful at all	Somewhat useful	Useful	Very Useful	IPs have applied research findings/products to activities
Climate-Resilient Cereals (i.e. CGIAR maize, wheat, and rice programs)								
Legume Productivity (i.e. Peanut and Mycotoxin Innovation Lab and Legume Innovation Lab)								
Advanced Approaches								

Research Program areas	Not aware of research products, findings, assistance or support in this program area	Have not drawn on resources related to this program area	Not relevant to our portfolio	Not useful at all	Somewhat useful	Useful	Very Useful	IPs have applied research findings/products to activities
to Combat Pests and Diseases (i.e. BT Cowpea and BT Eggplant)								
Research on Nutritious and Safe Foods (i.e. Nutrition and Horticulture Innovation Labs)								
Markets and Policy Research (i.e. AMA-BASIS Innovation Lab)								
Sustainable Intensification (i.e. Africa RISING)								
Human and Institutional Capacity Development (i.e. BHEARD)								

Comments:

22. To what extent do you feel that the various research projects in this country are integrated with the overall Feed the Future mission program?

       1 – Not at all

       2 - Not very well

       3 – Somewhat

       4 – Well integrated

       5 – Very well integrated

Comments:

23. To what extent do you feel that the various research projects in this country complement each other or build synergies?

       1 – Not at all

       2 - Not very well

       3 – Somewhat

       4 – Complementary

       5 – Very complimentary

Comments:

Centrally-managed Mechanisms

Centrally-managed mechanisms are intended to complement Mission programs and engagement by focusing on regional or global dimensions that improve the efficiency and effectiveness of mission programs. To improve the complementarity of USAID investment, mission vs central program roles must be balanced.

24. From your experience, how well have centrally-managed mechanisms contributed to your mission's efforts to achieve your goals and objectives?

Please check all that apply.

1	Central mechanisms **have not been** well-coordinated with the Mission.	

2	Central mechanisms have been well-coordinated with the Mission.	
3	Central mechanisms provide access to important activities for our portfolio.	
4	Central mechanisms reduce procurement burden on Missions.	
5	Central mechanisms **have not fit** the Mission's programmatic needs.	
6	Central mechanisms **have not contributed** to achieving our Feed the Future goals and objectives.	
7	We have not accessed central mechanisms.	

Comments:

Thank you very much for taking the time to respond to the questions in this survey.

INTRODUCTION

Thank you for taking out valuable time to respond to this survey. It is designed to obtain data for the Global Performance Evaluation of the Feed the Future Initiative. This survey was sent to Regional Mission Feed the Future Team Lead/Coordinators, and each mission can provide two responses (respondents) for the survey.

To minimize the time it takes to respond to this survey, the majority of the questions are designed as multiple choices for you to check off your responses. At the same time, we strongly encourage you to provide explanations to your answers in the comment box following every question as your ideas and feedback are important in informing modifications or adjustment to Feed the Future initiative.

1. Please select which Regional Mission you work with.

Monitoring, Evaluation and Learning Questions

The Feed the Future monitoring, evaluation and learning (MEL) approach is based on the Feed the Future Results Framework, which establishes the goals and objectives of the initiative; a performance monitoring process and standard performance indicators to track progress toward desired results; local human and institutional capacity-building investment to improve the quality and frequency of data collection and use; performance evaluations and impact evaluations to examine how programs are working and to determine the measurable effects of Feed the Future investments; and knowledge-sharing activities to foster learning and use of M&E findings.

2. How helpful have the Feed the Future Guide and M&E Guidance documents, support from BFS personnel, and BFS-managed M&E implementing mechanisms been in **clarifying the Feed the Future MEL approach and how to apply it**

Please check the response that applies to each resource listed in the left hand column of the table.

Resources	0 Not aware of this resource	1 Have not consulted/ Have not attended	2 Not helpful At all	3 Not very helpful	4 Somewhat helpful	5 Helpful	6 Very helpful
Feed the Future Guide 2010							
Results Framework document							
Vol. 1: M&E Under Feed the Future: MEL Approach							
Feed the Future Indicator Handbook							
Frequently Asked Questions: Feed the Future MEL Approach							
Support from BFS personnel							
Support from BFS-managed MEL mechanisms							
Other: Please write in							
Other: Please write in							
Other: Please write in							

Comments:

3. How helpful have Feed the Future documents from the M&E Guidance Series, other guidance documents, support from BFS personnel and support from BFS

MEL implementing mechanisms been in *clarifying how to collect and analyze data* for Feed the Future indicators?

Please check the response that applies to each resource listed in the left hand column in the table below.

Resources	0 Not aware of this	1 Not applicable	2 Have not used	3 Not helpful At all	4 Not very helpful	5 Somewhat helpful	6 Helpful	7 Very helpful
Feed the Future Indicator Handbook								
Feed the Future Agricultural Indicators Guide								
M&E Guidance Series Vol. 5: Measuring Local Capacity Development								
M&E Guidance Series Vol. 6: Measuring the Gender Impact of Feed the Future								
M&E Guidance Series Vol. 7: Measuring Natural Resources Management and Climate Change Resiliency								
Guide for applying Women's Empowerment in Agriculture Index (WEAI)								

Resources	0 Not aware of this	1 Not applicable	2 Have not used	3 Not helpful At all	4 Not very helpful	5 Somewhat helpful	6 Helpful	7 Very helpful
Feed the Future Gender Integration Framework								
BFS led training and workshops								
Support from BFS MEL implementing mechanisms								
Other: Please write in								
Other: Please write in								
Other: Please write in								

Comments:

4. How helpful is the Feed the Future standard indicator framework and FTFMS reporting in promoting achievements and accountability for Feed the Future commitments?

       13 Not helpful at all
       14 Not very helpful
       15 Somewhat helpful
       16 Helpful
       17 Very helpful
       18 Do not know

Comments:

5. How helpful is the development and application of the Feed the Future Learning Agenda in promoting achievements and accountability for Feed the Future commitments?

13 Not helpful at all
14 Not very helpful
15 Somewhat helpful
16 Helpful
17 Very helpful
18 Do not know

Comments:

6. How well do the indicators under the Feed the Future standard indicator framework/handbook enable your mission to track key objectives related to your program?

Please check all that apply.

1	The standard indicator framework provides useful indicators to track every key objective of our program.	
2	The standard indicator framework provides useful indicators to track most of the key objective of our program.	
3	The standard indicator framework **does not** provide useful indicators to track most of the key objective of our program.	
4	The standard indicator framework provides too many indicators.	
5	There are too many **required** indicators under the standard indicator framework.	
6	Most of the indicators included in the standard indicator framework are irrelevant to the objectives of our Feed the Future program.	
7	Many of the indicators included in the standard indicator framework are too difficult to measure or track.	

Comments:

7. How accurately does the Feed the Future Results Framework (RF) reflect the development hypotheses of your mission's program and the causal pathways that lead from Feed the Future programmatic outcomes to the goal of reducing poverty and stunting?

Please check all that apply.

1	The RF reflects all causal relationships in the development hypotheses underlying our Feed the Future program.	
2	The RF reflects most of the causal relationships of the development hypotheses of our program, but not all. Some relevant causal links are not represented.	
3	The RF does not reflect many aspects of the development hypotheses underlying our Feed the Future program. Many relevant causal links are missing.	
4	The RF includes causal relationships that are not relevant to the food security situation in the country where I work.	
5	Critical causal relationships related to agricultural growth are missing from the RF.	
6	Critical causal relationships related to nutrition are missing from the RF.	

Comments:

Value Chain Questions (if applicable)

8. How effective is the value chain approach employed by Feed the Future (targeting a limited number of value chain commodities and working through various links in the value chain) in achieving targeted goals and objectives?

Please check all that apply.

1	The value chain approach limited our ability to meet goals and/or objectives.	
2	The value chain approach effectively focused our resources.	
3	The value chain approach enabled our programs to meet goals and/or objectives.	
4	Focus on a value chain approach caused us to miss opportunities to meet our goals and/or objectives.	
5	The value chain approach could be effective, but our selection of specific value chains may have limited our ability to meet goals and/or objectives.	
6	More flexibility is needed in program design to meet Feed the Future goals.	

Comments:

Private Sector Questions

9. How many partnerships with private sector entities has the Mission developed to date to support agriculture or nutrition interventions?

Please write in the number.

Agriculture Interventions	Nutrition Interventions

Capacity Development Questions

10. What type of human and institutional capacity development (HICD) interventions have you implemented to date that have **succeeded** in increasing the capacity of your regional government partners to effectively undertake interventions related to their roles in the partnership in the agriculture and nutrition sectors and promoting regional and cross-border trade?

Please check all that apply		Agriculture sector	Nutrition sector	Regional harmonization of trade /food safety policies, tariffs, regulations
0	On-the-job training (OJT)			
1	Mentoring			
2	Workshops:			
3	Improving information systems			
	Training to increase data collection and analytical capabilities (use of information systems)			
4	Improving ICT capabilities			
5	New or replacement equipment			
6	Funding for facility upgrades			
7	Other: Please write in			
8	Other: Please write in			
9	Other Please write in			

Comments:

11. Have you had assistance from BFS centrally managed HICD activities to increase staff capacity in any of the partnering regional or local institutions or organizations?

> 0 = No
>
> 1 = Yes

Please skip to question 12 if your answer is no

Comments:

12. Was that assistance well-coordinated with the regional mission's **own efforts to** increase capacity?

> 1 = Not at all coordinated with Mission-identified HICD needs
>
> 2 = Not very well coordinated
>
> 3 = Somewhat
>
> 4 = Coordinated
>
> 5 = Very Well Coordinated

Comments:

Regional Policy Intervention Questions

13. Which Feed the Future Focus Countries in the region benefit from the Mission's work in promoting cross-border and regional trade?

Please list in the table below.

Comments:

14. Has the Mission's promotion of regional/trans-border reforms to date made a positive contribution toward bilateral Mission progress in meeting targets for any of the following Feed the Future indicators?

Please check your response for each of the following Feed the Future indicators and include the name/s of the Mission for all "yes" responses

Feed the Future Indicators		Mission	Yes	No	N/A
	Gross margin per hectare, animal or cage of selected product (from availability of agricultural inputs from the region to value chain actors)				
2	Value of intra-regional trade in agricultural commodities				
3	Value of exports for targeted agricultural commodities				
4	Value of incremental sales				
5	Number of jobs				
6	Number of national-level policies required for full implementation of a regionally agreed-upon policy progressing through necessary steps as a result of USG assistance				
7	Other: please write in				
8	Other: please write in				

Feed the Future Indicators		Mission	Yes	No	N/A
9	Other: please write in				
10	No contributions to meeting targets in any Feed the Future indicators the Bilateral Mission/s report on				

Comments:

Learning Questions

15. Have you used Feed the Future learning products in any of the following thematic areas?

Please check your response for each of the thematic areas listed across the top of the table.

Thematic Areas	Improved Agricultural Productivity	Improved Research & Development	Expanded Markets, Value Chains & Increased Investment	Improved Nutrition & Dietary Quality	Improved Gender Integration & Women's Empowerment	Improved Resilience of Vulnerable Populations
0 – I am not aware of any of learning products related to this theme						
1 – I am aware of learning products related to this theme but have not examined them						
2 – I have looked at learning products from this theme but there are no findings that can be applied to our program						

Thematic Areas	Improved Agricultural Productivity	Improved Research & Development	Expanded Markets, Value Chains & Increased Investment	Improved Nutrition & Dietary Quality	Improved Gender Integration & Women's Empowerment	Improved Resilience of Vulnerable Populations
3 – We are discussing some of the actionable lessons learned among members of our Feed the Future team and/or partners						
4- We have applied some of the actionable lessons learned to our Feed the Future activities but it is too early to determine the benefit to support Feed the Future program outcomes and goals.						
5. We have attempted to apply some of the actionable lessons learned to our Feed the Future activities but found implementation was not practical or cost-efficient for our country program.						
6. We have applied some of the actionable lessons learned to our Feed the Future activities and there is some						

Thematic Areas	Improved Agricultural Productivity	Improved Research & Development	Expanded Markets, Value Chains & Increased Investment	Improved Nutrition & Dietary Quality	Improved Gender Integration & Women's Empowerment	Improved Resilience of Vulnerable Populations
indication that it will prove beneficial to the Feed the Future program.						

Comments:

16. In what ways does your Mission Feed the Future team use Agrilinks?

Please check all that apply.

1	To learn about recent innovations that may be useful/applicable to our program	
2	To learn about upcoming training opportunities and webinars	
3	To access resources useful for the design of new Feed the Future activities	
4	To participate in groups (e.g. Agriculture and Nutrition Global Learning and Evidence Exchange, Extension and Advisory Services Group, etc.)	
5	To share experiences and lessons learned in blogs	
6	To learn about upcoming events (e.g. Agriculture Sector Council Seminars)	
7	Our team does not use Agrolinks.	
8	Other: Please write in	

Comments:

17. What resources has the Mission Feed the Future team found to be valuable that were sourced from the Agrilinks website?

Please check all that apply.

1	Links to webinars	
2	Blogs	
3	Groups	
4	Notice of upcoming events such as Ag Sector Council Seminars	

5	Reports on recent research findings	
6	Articles on how to implement cross-cutting activities such as climate smart agriculture, nutrition sensitive agriculture, gender, etc.	
7	Recent evaluations related to Feed the Future topics	
8	Other: Please write in	
9	Other: Please write in	
10	None	

Comments:

Research Questions

The Feed the Future Research Strategy is organized around seven key challenge (program) areas related to sustainably transforming agricultural production systems, ensuring access to nutritious and safe foods, creating enabling and supportive policies, and addressing the emerging challenges of climate change and natural resources scarcity. Feed the Future research may be funded through a variety of mechanisms including Innovation Labs with U.S. Universities, cooperative agreements with private companies, and various CGIAR grants –such as Africa RISING and Bio-safety programs.

18. How useful are the research products, technical assistance and support offered in each program area through the Feed the Future centrally-managed research mechanisms in contributing to agriculture and nutrition outcomes in this country?

Please check responses for each program area listed in the left hand column.

Research Program areas	Not aware of research products, findings, assistance or support in this program area	Have not drawn on resources related to this program area	Not relevant to our Feed the Future portfolio	Not useful at all	Somewhat useful	Useful	Very Useful	IPs have applied research findings/products to Feed the Future activities
Climate-Resilient Cereals (i.e. CGIAR maize, wheat, and rice programs)								
Legume Productivity (i.e. Peanut and Mycotoxin Innovation Lab and Legume Innovation Lab)								
Advanced Approaches to Combat Pests and Diseases (i.e. BT Cowpea and BT Eggplant)								
Research on Nutritious								

Research Program areas	Not aware of research products, findings, assistance or support in this program area	Have not drawn on resources related to this program area	Not relevant to our Feed the Future portfolio	Not useful at all	Somewhat useful	Useful	Very Useful	IPs have applied research findings/products to Feed the Future activities
and Safe Foods (i.e. Nutrition and Horticulture Innovation Labs)								
Markets and Policy Research (i.e. AMA-BASIS Innovation Lab)								
Sustainable Intensification (i.e. Africa RISING)								
Human and Institutional Capacity Development (i.e. BHEARD)								

Comments:

Centrally-managed Mechanisms

Centrally-managed mechanisms are intended to complement Mission programs and engagement by focusing on regional or global dimensions that improve the efficiency and effectiveness of mission programs. To improve the complementarity of USAID investment, mission vs central program roles must be balanced.

19. From your experience, how well have centrally-managed mechanisms contributed to your mission's efforts to achieve your goals and objectives?

Please check all that apply.

1	Central mechanisms **have not been** well-coordinated with the Mission.	
2	Central mechanisms have been well-coordinated with the Mission.	
3	Central mechanisms provide access to important activities for our portfolio.	
4	Central mechanisms reduce procurement burden on Missions.	
5	Central mechanisms **have not fit** the Mission's programmatic needs.	
6	Central mechanisms **have not contributed** to achieving our Feed the Future goals and objectives.	
7	We have not accessed central mechanisms.	

Comments:

Thank you very much for taking the time to respond to the questions in this survey.

a. Bibliography

"500+ Top State Leaders on Capitol Hill Today to Urge Congressional Support of International Affairs Budget." June 14, 2016. http://www.usglc.org/2016/06/14/500-top-state-leaders-on-capitol-hill-today-to-urge-congressional-support-of-international-affairs-budget/. Accessed June 24, 2016.

"2011 GLOBAL EDUCATION WORKSHOP: FROM EVIDENCE TO ACTION." Powerpoint presented at the GLOBAL EDUCATION WORKSHOP: FROM EVIDENCE TO ACTION. Arlington, VA ; August 22-25, 2011.

2015 Achieving Impact: Leadership and Partnership to Feed the Future. USAID, Bureau of Food Security. Washington, DC. 2015.

2015 USAID Forward Results: Strengthening Local Capacity Data Table. USAID. Retrieved 29 June 2016 from https://www.usaid.gov/usaidforward.

"A Landscape Analysis of Activities in 19 Focus Countries." Roslyn, John Snow, Inc, SPRING. 2014.

"A Short Guide to Pro-Poor Value Chain Program Design." Melbourne, Action for Enterprise. 2013.

"A Synthesis of Making Markets Work for the Poor (M4P) Approach." DiFD.

Adams, Lawrencia, and Cecilia Addae. "Organizational Capacity Assessment Report. Ghana National Association of Farmers And Fishermen (GNAFF)." December 2014.

"Agroecology: The Ecology of Food Systems", Francis, C., G. Lieblein, S. Gliessman, T.A. Breland, N. Creamer, R. Harwood, L. Salomonsson, J. Helenius, D. Rickerl, R. Salvador, M. Wiendehoeft, S. Simmons, P. Allen, M. Altieri, J. Porter, C. Flora, and R. Poincelot. Journal of Sustainable Agriculture 22:99-118. 2003.

Alkire, Sabina, et. Al. "The Women's Empowerment in Agriculture Index." International Food and Policy Research Institute, 2012.

Altenburg, Tilman. "Donor Approaches to Supporting Pro-Poor Value Chains." Report prepared for the Donor Committee for Enterprise Development Working Group on Linkages and Value Chains. Bonn, German Development Institute. 2007.

"Assessing the Feed the Future Initiative" - The Center for Global Development. March 2016. Berhane, Gussh, et al. "Evaluation of Ethiopia's Food Security Program: Documenting Progress in the Implementation of the Productive Safety Nets Programme and the Household Asset Building Programme." Washington, DC, IFPRI. 2013.

Bhutta, Z., Das, J., Rizvi, A., Gaffey, M., Walker, N., & Horton, S. et al. (2013). Evidence-based interventions for improvement of maternal and child nutrition: what can be done and at what cost? *The Lancet, 382*(9890), 452-477. http://dx.doi.org/10.1016/s0140-6736(13)60996-4.

Brache, I. "The New Alliance for Food Security and Nutrition: A Turning Point?" EU Report. 2015.

"Building Institutional Capacity to Increase Food Security in Africa." Food Security Collaborative. April 2012.

"Building Resilience to Recurrent Crisis: USAID Policy and Program Guidance." Washington, DC, USAID. 2012.

Burruss, Duke, Ndidi Nwuneli and Kwesi Opoku-Debrah. "Feed the Future (FTF) Institutional Mapping and Assessment." Africa LEAD. January 25, 2012.

"Capacity Development: A UNDP Primer." United Nations Development Programme. 2009.

The Challenge of Capacity Development- Working Towards Good Practice. OECD-DAC. 2006.

"Characterization of farming systems in Africa RISING intervention sites in Malawi, Tanzania, Ghana and Mali." http://africa-rising.net/

"The Cost of Hunger in Malawi." May 2015. http://reliefweb.int/sites/reliefweb.int/files/resources/wfp274603.pdf

"The Cost of Hunger in Uganda." 2013. http://npa.ug/wp-content/themes/npatheme/documents/Publications/Cost%20of%20Hunger%20report%20summary%20version_Final%20Edition.pdf

Country Ownership: Moving From Rhetoric to Action." Washington, DC, Interaction. 2011.

Crawford, Eric, Isaac Minde, Kathleen Colverson, Russell Freed, and Steven Haggblade. "Assessment of Needs for Training, Collaborative Research, and Institutional Capacity Building for Agricultural Development and Food Security in Tanzania iAGRI Report Series, No. 1. The Ohio State University Consortium. December, 2011.

"Declaration of the World Summit on Food Security." Rome, World Summit on Food Security. 2009.

Dichter, Thomas, David Joslyn, Joyce L. Moock, and M. Diane Bellis. "Feed the Future Human and Institutional Capacity Development Strategy Review." USAID. May 8, 2015.

Elliot, Kimberly and Casey Dunning. "Assessing the US Feed the Future Initiative: A New Approach to Food Security." Washington, DC, Center for Global Development. 2016.

Energizing Champions for Food Security: Reflections on What Works, Why, and What are the Challenges." Africa LEAD. April 2013.

FACT Sheet: The New Alliance for Food Security and Nutrition. White House press release. June 18 2013.

FAO. "The State of Food and Agriculture – Women in Agriculture (2010-11)." 2011.

Feed the Future AgriLinks. "Increasing Fee the Future Impacts through Targeted Gender Integration."   https://agrilinks.org/events/increasing-feed-future-impacts-through-targeted-gender-integration.

Feed the Future. "Civil Society Action Plan." May 2014.

"Feed the Future Guide." Washington, DC. USAID/BFS. 2010.

Feed the Future Guidance for Setting Targets for Zone of Influence Population-Based Indicators and for Percent Growth in Agricultural GDP indicator: Per Capita Expenditures, Exclusive Breastfeeding/Minimum Adequate Diet and Anemia guidance revised. USAID. April 2013.

"Feed the Future Guide to Supporting Sound Policy Enabling Environments." US Government Interagency. August 16, 2013.

Feed the Future Indicator Handbook: Definition Sheets (updated October 18, 2013). USAID.

Feed the Future Learning Agenda Literature Review: Improved Gender Integration and Women's Empowerment, USAID. June 23, 2015.

Feed the Future M&E Guidance Series Vol. 6: Measuring the Gender Impact of FTF. 2014.

Final Evaluation Report The Haiti Title II Multi-year Assistance Programs (MYAP) Final Evaluation Report. 2014.

Food for the Hungry—Mozambique: P.L. 480 Title II Multi-year Assistance Program Final Evaluation. 2013.

"Food Security Country Framework for Ethiopia." Washington, DC. USAID/FFP. 2015.

"Food Security Desk Review for Mali: FY 2015-2019." Washington, DC, USAID/FFP. 2015.

FOREIGN AID: USAID Has Increased Funding to Partner Country Organizations but Could Better Track Progress. 2014. GAO. Retrieved on 6 July 2016 from http://www.gao.gov/assets/670/662596.pdf.

"Energizing Champions for Food Security: Reflections on What Works, Why, And What Are The Challenges." Africa Lead. April 2013.

Gary, George; Laura Kuhl and Demese Chanyalew. "External Mid-Term Performance Evaluation Report: Feed the Future Ethiopia" Washington, DC, USAID/BFS. 2015.

Gelli, Aulo and Hawkes, Corinna and Donovan, Jason and Harris, Jody and Allen, Summer L. and de Brauw, Alan and Henson, Spencer and Johnson, Nancy and Garrett, James and Ryckembusch, David, Value Chains and Nutrition: A Framework to Support the Identification, Design, and Evaluation of Interventions (January 30, 2015). IFPRI Discussion Paper 01413. http://ssrn.com/abstract=2564541 orhttp://dx.doi.org/10.2139/ssrn.2564541

Gerrard, Chris, Gem Argwings-Kodhek, Ali Marouani, and Godfrey Mudimu. "Independent Evaluation of CAADP Multi-Donor Trust Fund (MDTF)." Volume 1: Main Report. April 9, 2016.

"The Grow Africa partnership", in Development Co-operation Report 2015: Making Partnerships Effective Coalitions for Action, OECD Publishing, Paris. 2015. DOI: http://dx.doi.org/10.1787/dcr-2015-22-en

"Growing Innovation, Harvesting Results." Feed the Future Progress Report. Washington, DC, USAID. 2013.

Ingram, G. M., &Biau, J. The Brookings Institution. *A Data Picture of USAID Public-Private Partnerships: 2001 – 2014*. October 2014. Retrieved June 5, 2016, from https://www.usaid.gov/opengov/developer/datasets/Ingram_PPP_Fact_Sheet_Final.pdf.

International Livestock Research Institute and International Institute of Tropical Agriculture. 2013. "Africa RISING program framework: Core elements." Africa RISING Brief 2. Nairobi, Kenya: International Livestock Research Institute.

Hanaran, Charles. Global Food Security by the Numbers. The Chicago Council on Foreign Affairs. September 2015.

Heather Baser and Peter Morgan. "Capacity, Change, and Performance." Discussion Paper No. 59B. European Center for Development Policy Management (ECDPM). April 2008.

Hervy, Anne-Claire and Andrew Gilboy. "Good Practices in Leveraging Long-term Training for Institutional Capacity Strengthening." Association for Public and Land-grant Universities, Knowledge Center on Higher Education for African Development. February 2014.

"Independent Assessment of the CAADP Multi-Donor Trust Fund." Discussion paper no. 158. ECDPM, ESRF, and LARES. February 2014.

Innovation Lab for Nutrition- Africa Annual Report October 1st, 2014- September 30th, 2015.

Irene Annor-Frempong. "Human and Institutional Capacity Development Strategy Review: African Stakeholder Perspectives." Feed the Future. May 15, 2015.

Karen J. Jansen, Kevin G. Corley, K., and Bernard J. Jansen. "E-Survey Methodology." Chapter 1, in "Handbook of Research on Electronic Surveys and Measurements," by Rodney A. Reynolds, Robert Woods and Jason D. Baker. IGI Global: 2007.

Kessy, Flora, ed. "Translating Growth into Poverty Reduction: Beyond the Numbers." Dar-es-Salaam, Mkuki Na Nyota. 2013.

Kolavalli, Shashidhara and Regina Birner. "The Comprehensive Africa Agriculture Development Programme as a Collective Institution."Discussion note # 005. IFPRI/Ghana Strategy Support Program, paper presented at the Transforming Agriculture Conference, 8-9 November 2012.

Landscape Analysis of Activities Across 19 Focus Countries: Linking Agriculture and Nutrition. SPRING. USAID. June 2014.

Lawson, Marian L., Randy Schnepf, and Nicolas Cook. "The Obama Administration's Feed the Future Initiative." Congressional Research Service. 2016.

Lechtenberg, Victor, Albert Ayeni, Ralph Christy, and Carol Kramer-LeBlanc, Consultant "BIFAD Strategic Human and Institutional Capacity Development (HICD) Issue s and the Role of USAID and Title XII." March 2014.

"Leveraging Agriculture for Nutrition Impact through the Feed the Future Initiative: A Landscape Analysis of Activities Across 19 Focus Countries." SPRING. June 2014.

"Linking Agriculture to Nutrition: A Guide to Context Assessment tools." Roslyn, John Snow, Inc, SPRING. 2014.

Lopez, J Humberto (2006). "Pro-Poor Growth: A Reivew of What We Know (and What We Don't). Washington, DC, World Bank, PRMPR; and: Feed the Future Tool for Targeting. 2011.

"M&E Guidance Series Volume 1: Monitoring and Evaluation Under Feed The Future." Feed the Future. Undated.

Malapit, Hazel Jean, et. Al. "Measuring Progress toward Empowerment – Women's Empowerment in Agriculture Index: Baseline Report." 2014.

Malawi Portfolio Review Presentation, FY 2015.

Man Tlachan, Pradeep, et al. "Value Chain Analysis of Rice Seeds in Bangladesh: A Case of Three Southern Districts: Jessore, Khulna and Barisal." Dacca, International Rice Research Institute. 2012.

Marc J. Cohen. "U.S. Aid to Agriculture: Shifting Focus from Production to Sustainable Food Security." The Penn State Journal of Law & International Affairs, Vol. 3, Issue 2.2015. Available at: http://elibrary.law.psu.edu/jlia/vol3/iss2/8

Marian L. Lawson, Randy Schnepf, and Nicolas Cook. "The Obama Administration's Feed the Future Initiative." Congressional Research Service. January 29, 2016.

McGregor S, Cheung YB, Cueto S, Glewwe P, Richter L, Strupp B; International Child Development Steering Group. Developmental potential in the first 5 years for children in developing countries. Lancet. 2007.

"Mid-Term Performance Evaluation of the Cambodia Harvest Project (Helping Address Rural Vulnerabilities and Ecosystem Stability." Washington, DC, USAID, BFS. 2013.
Mid-term evaluation of the Timbuktu food security initiative, USAID Mali. 2011.

"Modernizing Extension and Advisory Services (MEAS) Project." USAID. Undated. Retrieved from: http://pdf.usaid.gov/pdf_docs/pdacu599.pdf.

Ngo, T.M-P. & Wahhaj, Z. Microfinance and gender empowerment. Journal of Development Economics, 99(1). 2012.

OECD, "Data warehouse", OECD Stat (database). 2016.
DOI: http://dx.doi.org/10.1787/data-00900-en (Accessed on July 3, 2016)

OECD, *Geographical Distribution of Financial Flows to Developing Countries 2016: Disbursements, Commitments, Country Indicators*, OECD Publishing, Paris. 2016.
DOI: http://dx.doi.org/10.1787/fin_flows_dev-2016-en-fr

"Operating Guide for the Making Markets Work for the Poor Approach." SDC. 2014.

P. van Asten, 2015. Poverty and Maize - an intimate relationship. IITA presentation at USAID-Feed the Future offices in Uganda on 4 Dec 2015, 25 PowerPoint slides, unpublished.

PACT. "Introduction to Organizational Capacity Development: Pact Organizational Development Toolkit." January, 2010.

"The Paris Declaration on Aid Effectiveness: Five Principles for Smart Aid." OECD. 2008.

Pearson, Jenny. "Training and Beyond: Seeking Better Practices for Capacity Development." OECD Development Co-operation Working Papers No. 1. OECD/DAC publishing. 04-Apr-2011.

"Pathways Out of Poverty: Applying Key Principles of the Value Chain Approach to Reach the Very Poor." Washington, DC, USAID, MicroLinks Report 173.

Poulton, Colin, KassahunBerhanu, Blessings Chinsinga, Brian Cooksey, Frederick Golooba-Mutebi, and Augustin Loada "The Comprehensive Africa Agriculture Development Programme (CAADP): Political Incentives, Value Added and Ways Forward. Working Paper 077." Future Agricultures. February 2014.

"Pro-Poor Value Chain Development: 25 Guiding Questions for Designing and Implementing Agroindustry Projects." Vienna, UN Industrial Development Organization, IFAD and DIIS. 2011.

"Process Evaluation of the Peace Corps/Senegal Master Farmer Program." USAID Senegal. October 2014.

"Program for Human and Institutional Capacity Development." Fact Sheet. Feed the Future. Undated. Retrieved from: https://feedthefuture.gov/sites/default/files/resource/files/ftf_factsheet_fsiccapacity_oct2014.pdf.

Reichle, Susan. USAID Forward Strategic Overview. http://www.macf.com/images/stories/pdf/ASHA/2015/Plenary_Sessions/USAID-ASHA_2015_AC_-_USAID_Forward.pdf

Rey, Sally. Feed the Future AgriLinks Blog: "How does Feed the Future measure gender impacts?" https://agrilinks.org/blog/how-does-feed-future-measure-gender-impacts.

Sanogo, Issa and Joyce K Luma "An Assessment of the Impacts of the Global Economic Crises on Household Food Security: Innovative Approaches, Lessons and Challenges, Rome, WFP.

Save the Children Bangladesh Mid-term Review of NoboJibon Multi-year Assistance Program. 2013.

Simister, Nigel and with Rachel Smith. "Monitoring and Evaluating Capacity Building: Is it really that difficult?" Praxis Paper 23. International NGO Training Training and Research Centre (INTRAC). January 2010.

Snapp, S.S., P.L. Mafongoya, and S. Waddington. "Organic matter technologies for integrated nutrient management in smallholder farming systems of southern Africa." 1998.

Susanna B. Hecht. "The Evolution of Agroecological Thought," in Agroecology: The Scientific Basis of Alternative Agriculture, ed. by Miguel Altieri (Boulder CO: Westview Press, 1987), p. 4. NAL Call

S589.7.A4. Retrieved from: https://www.nal.usda.gov/afsic/sustainable-agriculture-definitions-and-terms-related-terms#term1.

"Surviving Shocks in Ethiopia: The Role of Social Protection for Food Security" in Pinstrup-Andersen, Per, ed. Food Policy for Developing Countries: the Role of Government in the Global Food System, Washington, DC, IFPRI. 2007.

"Synthesis of Evaluations Related to the Feed the Future Learning Agenda." Washington, DC, USAID/BFS. 2016.

Title II Food Security Program, PROMASA, Save the Children, MYAP 2006-2011: Endline Report, USAID Guatemala. 2011.

Tony Land, Volker Hauck and Heather Baser. Capacity Development: Between Planned Interventions and Emergent Processes: Implications for Development Cooperation." Policy Management Brief 22, European Center for Development Policy Management (ECDPM). March 2009.

"The Global Social Crisis (2011)." United Nations. 2011.

TS Jayne, A Chapoto, N Sitko, M Muyanga, C Nkonde and J Chamberlin. "Africa's Changing Farm Structure and Employment Challenge." Policy Synthesis, No. 9. Washington, DC, USAID. 2014.

Tumavick, Nancy M., and ASM Jahangir. "Final Draft: Feed the Future Report on Dialogue and Support for Policies Advancing Food Security, Agricultural Growth, and Better Nutrition." Feed the Future. March 30, 2016.

"Understanding and Applying Primary Pathways and Principles." Roslyn, John Snow, Inc, SPRING. 2014.

USAID. "Assessment of the Portfolio of the USAID/BFS Policy Division." March 2016.

USAID, Building Resilience to Recurrent Crisis, USAID Policy and Program Guidance, December 2012.

USAID. "Challenges Encountered in Capacity Building: Review of Literature and Selected Tools." Position paper no. 10. Management Sciences for Health, AIDS Support and Technical Assistance Resources. April 2010.

USAID. Data Quality Assessments for Feed the Future Indicators. March 21, 2014. https://agrilinks.org/sites/default/files/resource/files/Consolidated DQA PPT.pdfhttps://agrilinks.org/sites/default/files/resource/files/Consolidated DQA PPT.pdf

USAID. "Feed the Future Human and Institutional Capacity Development Strategy Review." May 8, 2015.

USAID. "Feed the Future Learning Agenda Literature Review: Improved Gender Integration and Women's Empowerment." January 2015.

USAID. "Honduras: Nutrition Profile." https://www.usaid.gov/sites/default/files/documents/1864/USAID-Honduras-Profile.pdf.

USAID. "Human and Institutional Capacity Development Handbook." October, 2010.

USAID. "Institutional Architecture for Food Security Policy Change: Cross-Country Study." March 2015.

USAID. Program for Research on Sustainable Intensification Strategy Overview and Vision Document, March 2016.

USAID. "Sustainable intensification of key farming systems in East and Southern Africa: Africa RISING Technical Report." 01 October 2015 to 31 March 2016.

USAID. Synthesis of Evaluation Related to the Feed the Future Learning Agenda. 2016.

USAID Forward Progress Report 2013. Retrieved 28 June 2016 from: https://www.usaid.gov/sites/default/files/documents/1868/2013-usaid-forward-report.pdfhttps://www.usaid.gov/sites/default/files/documents/1868/2013-usaid-forward-report.pdf

USAID Office of Market and Partnership Innovation Annual Portfolio Review, April 6, 2016.

USAID Public-Private Partnership Search Tool. Office of Global Development Alliance. Retrieved July 5, 2016, fromhttps://partnerships.usaid.gov/

USAID/Malawi Strategy Change Memorandum, October 1, 2015.

USAID/Rwanda Strategy Change Memorandum, November 9, 2015.

USAID/Uganda Strategy Change Memorandum, November 17, 2015.

Volume 5: USAID Forward/IPR and Feed the Future, March 2014. Retrieved 28 June 2016, from https://www.feedthefuture.gov/sites/default/files/resource/files/ftf_guidanceseries_vol5_localcapacitydevelopment_march2014.pdf

Volume 8: Population-Based Survey Instrument for Feed the Future Zone of Influence Indicators with Revised WEAI Module, October 2012. (pg. 4) Retrieved 21 June 2016, from https://www.feedthefuture.gov/sites/default/files/resource/files/ftf_vol8_populationbasedsurveyinstrument_oct2012.pdf.

Volume 9: Target Setting for Reduction in Prevalence of Poverty, Underweight and Stunting in Feed the Future Zones of Influence, March 2012. Retrieved 21 June 2016, from http://usaidprojectstarter.org/sites/default/files/resources/pdfs/ftf_volume9_targetsettingguidance_0.pdf.

Volume 11: Guidance On The First Interim Assessment Of The Feed The Future Zone Of Influence Population level Indicators, Revised October 2014. Retrieved 4 July 2016 from https://www.feedthefuture.gov/sites/default/files/resource/files/ftf_guidanceseries_vol11_interim_assessment_oct2014.pdf

Watson, David. "Monitoring and Evaluation of Capacity and Capacity Development. Discussion paper No. 58B." European Centre for Development Policy Management (ECDPM). April 2006.

Wellness and Agriculture for Life Advancement (WALA): Mid-term Evaluation Report, USAID Malawi. 2012.

Wiggins, Steve; Sharada Keats and Julia Compton. "What Caused the Food Price Spike of 2007/2008? Lessons For World Cereals Markets." Overseas Development Institute (ODI). 2010.

"Women in agriculture: Closing the Gender Gap." International Food Policy Research Institute. *Global Food Policy Report*. Washington, D.C. 2012.

Women Thrive Worldwide. "Gender in Feed the Future." http://www.womenthrive.org/sites/default/files/images/agriculture%20genderscan.pdf.

The World Bank. "World Development Report 2012: Gender Equality and Development." 2011.

"World Bank Development Report." Washington, DC, World Bank. 2008.

World Resources Institute. Installment 4 of "Creating a Sustainable Food Future: Improving land and water management. Robert Winterbottom et al. October 2013.

b. Interviews Conducted

FIELDWORK INTERVIEWS

Country	Office/Organization/ Institution Name	Office/Organization/ Institution Type	Number Interviewed
Bangladesh	Feed the Future Mission Team	USAID/Bangladesh	9
Bangladesh	Feed the Future M&E Team	USAID/Bangladesh	2
Bangladesh	Food For Peace (FFP)Team	USAID/Bangladesh	2
Bangladesh	Accelerating Capacity for Monitoring and Evaluation (ACME) Project - IBTCI	3rd Party M&E Contractor	3
Bangladesh	National Nutrition Services - Institute of Public Health	Focus Country Government	3
Bangladesh	Ministry of Food	Focus Country Government	3
Bangladesh	Strengthening Partnerships, Results, and Innovations in Nutrition Globally (SPRING) Project - JSI	Implementing Partner	2
Bangladesh	Agricultural Value Chains (AVC) Project - DAI	Implementing Partner	1
Bangladesh	Agriculture Extension Support Activity - Dhaka Ahsania Mission	Implementing Partner	1
Bangladesh	Accelerating Agriculture Productivity Improvement (AAPI) Project - IFDC	Implementing Partner	1
Bangladesh	Agro-Inputs (AIP) Project -CNFA	Implementing Partner	1
Bangladesh	Cereal Systems Initiative for South Asia- Mechanization and Irrigation (CSISA-MI)	Implementing Partner	1

Country	Office/Organization/ Institution Name	Office/Organization/ Institution Type	Number Interviewed
Bangladesh	SHIKHA - FHI360	Implementing Partner	1
Bangladesh	Policy Research and Strategy Support (PRSSP) Program - IFPRI	Implementing Partner	2
Bangladesh	International Rice Research Institute (IRRI)	Research Institution	1
Ghana	Feed the Future Mission Team	USAID/Ghana	10
Ghana	USAID/Ghana Tamale Office	USAID/Ghana	2
Ghana	Feed the Future Mission Team (M&E)	USAID/Ghana	5
Ghana	Peace Corps	Other USG/Field	5
Ghana	USDA	Other USG/Field	1
Ghana	Monitoring Evaluation and Technical Support Services (METTS) - Kansas State U	3rd Party M&E Contractor	4
Ghana	World Bank	Donor/Multilateral	1
Ghana	Ministry of Food and Agriculture (MoFA)	Focus Country Government	1
Ghana	Agricultural Development and Value Chain Enhancement (ADVANCE) Project -ACDI-VOCA	Implementing Partner	1
Ghana	Agriculture Technology Transfer (ATT) Project - IFDC	Implementing Partner	2
Ghana	Resiliency in Northern Ghana (RING) Project - Global Communities	Implementing Partner	4

Country	Office/Organization/ Institution Name	Office/Organization/ Institution Type	Number Interviewed
Ghana	Strengthening Partnerships, Results, and Innovations in Nutrition Globally (SPRING) Project - JSI	Implementing Partner	6
Ghana	Agricultural Development and Value Chain Enhancement (ADVANCE) Project -ACDI-VOCA (Tamale Office)	Implementing Partner	5
Ghana	Ghana Agriculture Policy Support (PSP) Project - Chemonics	Implementing Partner	2
Ghana	AfricaLead - DAI	Implementing Partner	2
Ghana	AGRA	Implementing Partner	2
Ghana	Financing Ghanaian Agriculture (FINGAP) Project - Carana	Implementing Partner	1
Ghana	Ghana Commercial Agriculture (GCAP) Project - MoFA	Implementing Partner	2
Ghana	Ghana Grains Council	Private Sector	2
Ghana	University of Development Studies (UDS)	Research Institution	1
Ghana	Savanna Agricultural Research Institute (SARI)	Research Institution	8
Guatemala	Feed the Future Mission Team	USAID/Guatemala	8
Guatemala	Feed the Future M&E Team	USAID/Guatemala	3
Guatemala	Food for Peace	USAID/Guatemala	2

Country	Office/Organization/Institution Name	Office/Organization/Institution Type	Number Interviewed
Guatemala	USDA	Other USG/Field	2
Guatemala	DevTech	3rd Party M&E Contractor	2
Guatemala	World Food Program	Donor/Multilateral	2
Guatemala	Ministry of Agriculture	Focus Country Government	1
Guatemala	Secretariat for Food Security and Nutrition (SESAN)	Focus Country Government	1
Guatemala	Food and Nutrition Technical Assistance (FANTA) - FHI360	Implementing Partner	2
Guatemala	Farmer-to-Farmer (F2F) - Partners of the Americas	Implementing Partner	1
Guatemala	NexosLocales - DAI	Implementing Partner	3
Guatemala	Cooperative Development Program II (CDP-III) - NCBA CLUSA	Implementing Partner	2
Guatemala	Buena Milpa - CIMMYT	Implementing Partner	2
Guatemala	Mas Frijol - Michigan State University	Implementing Partner	3
Guatemala	Fundaeco	Implementing Partner	1
Guatemala	Rural Value Chains Project -AGEXPORT	Implementing Partner	5

Country	Office/Organization/ Institution Name	Office/Organization/ Institution Type	Number Interviewed
Guatemala	Rural Value Chains Project -Anacafé/Funcafé	Implementing Partner	4
Guatemala	Food Security Focused on the First Thousand Days (SEGAMIL) Project - CRS	Implementing Partner (FFP DFAP)	2
Guatemala	Programa de Acciones Integradas de Seguridad Alimentaria y Nutricional del Occidente (PAISANO) - Save the Children	Implementing Partner (FFP DFAP)	1
Guatemala	Fair Fruit	Local Private Sector Partner (P4I/Fintrac)	1
Malawi	U.S. Embassy POC for USDA, OPIC, Treasury, and Commerce	Other USG/Field	1
Malawi	Feed the Future Mission Team	USAID/Malawi	5
Malawi	Feed the Future Mission Team (M&E)	USAID/Malawi	3
Malawi	Food For Peace Team	USAID/Malawi	2
Malawi	Donor Coordination Committee for Agriculture and Food Security (DCAFS)	Donor/Multilateral	1
Malawi	National Agricultural Research Service (NARS)	Focus Country Government	1
Malawi	National Agricultural Extension Service (NAES)	Focus Country Government	1
Malawi	Integrating Nutrition in Value Chains (INVC) Project - DAI	Implementing Partner	5
Malawi	Mobile Money Project -FHI360	Implementing Partner	3

Country	Office/Organization/ Institution Name	Office/Organization/ Institution Type	Number Interviewed
Malawi	Njira Project - PCI	Implementing Partner	3
Malawi	New Alliance Policy Acceleration Support (NAPAS) Project- Michigan State U	Implementing Partner	1
Malawi	Malawi Agriculture Policy Strengthening (MAPS) Project - Farmers Union of Malawi	Implementing Partner	2
Malawi	Strengthening Agriculture and Nutrition Extension (SANE) Project - U of Illinois	Implementing Partner	1
Malawi	Strengthening Evidence-Based Agriculture Policy (SEBAP) Project -IFPRI	Implementing Partner	2
Malawi	AGRA	Implementing Partner	1
Malawi	Agricultural Innovations Project (AIP) - Cornell U	Implementing Partner	1
Malawi	Malawi Improved Seed Systems and Technologies (MISST) Project - ICRISAT	Implementing Partner	1
Malawi	Ubale Project (CRS)	Implementing Partner (FFP DFAP)	2
Malawi	Lilongwe University of Agriculture and Natural Resources (LUANAR)	Local Implementing Partner (AIP Project)	1
Malawi	National Smallholder Farmers Association of Malawi (NASFAM)	Local Implementing Partner (INVC Project)	1
Malawi	Malawi Opportunity Bank	Local Private Sector Partner (Fintrac-P4I)	1
Malawi	Agriculture Commodity Exchange for Africa (ACE)	Local Private Sector Partner (INVC Project)	1

Country	Office/Organization/ Institution Name	Office/Organization/ Institution Type	Number Interviewed
Malawi	Peacock Seeds	Local Private Sector Partner (MISST Project)	1
Uganda	Feed the Future Mission Team	USAID/Uganda	13
Uganda	Feed the Future Mission Team (M&E)	USAID/Uganda	3
Uganda	DANIDA	Donor/Multilateral	1
Uganda	World Bank	Donor/Multilateral	1
Uganda	DFID	Donor/Multilateral	2
Uganda	IrishAid	Donor/Multilateral	1
Uganda	World Food Program	Donor/Multilateral	1
Uganda	Ministry of Agriculture	Focus Country Government	2
Uganda	Uganda Community Connector Project - FHI360	Implementing Partner	5
Uganda	NUCAFE	Implementing Partner	4
Uganda	aBi Trust	Implementing Partner	8
Uganda	HarvestPlus	Implementing Partner	2
Uganda	Commodity Production & Marketing (CPM) Activity - Chemonics	Implementing Partner	4

Country	Office/Organization/ Institution Name	Office/Organization/ Institution Type	Number Interviewed
Uganda	Agricultural Inputs Activity - Tetra Tech	Implementing Partner	1
Uganda	Enabling Environment for Agriculture Activity - Tetra Tech	Implementing Partner	1
Uganda	Northern Karamoja Growth, Health and Governance (GHG) Project -Mercy Corps	Implementing Partner (FFP DFAP)	3
Uganda	National Agricultural Research Organization (NARO)	Research Institution	1
Uganda	International Institute for Tropical Agriculture (IITA)	Research Institution	1

Organization Type	Organization/Office Name	Number Interviewed
USAD/BFS	Agriculture Research and Policy (ARP) - Program for HICD	1
USAID/BFS	Agriculture Research and Policy (ARP) - Policy Division	7
USAID/BFS	Agriculture Research and Policy (ARP) - Research Division	5
USAID/BFS	Bureau for Food Security(BFS)	6
USAID/BFS	Office of Global Engagement Strategy	1
USAID/BFS	Office of Resilience	1
USAID/BFS	Country Strategies and Implementation (CSI)	3
USAID/BFS	Markets, Partnerships and Innovations (MPI)	5
USAID/BFS	Monitoring Evaluation, and Learning (MEL) Team	8
USAID/DCHA	Food for Peace (FFP)	2
USAID/E3	Economic Growth Team	2
USAID/Mozambique	Economic Growth Team	1
USAID/Zimbabwe	Economic Growth Team	1

Organization Type	Organization/Office Name	Number Interviewed
Other USG	Department of Commerce	1
Other USG	Department of Treasury	1
Other USG	OPIC	1
Other USG	Millennium Challenge Corporation	5
Other USG	Peace Corps	2
Other USG	US African Development Foundation	5
Innovation Lab	Innovation Lab Food Security Policy	1
Innovation Lab	Innovation Lab for Aquaculture and Fish	1
Innovation Lab	Innovation Lab for Heat Tolerant Wheat	1
Innovation Lab	Innovation Lab for Legumes	1
Innovation Lab	Innovation Lab for Nutrition	1
Innovation Lab	Innovation Lab for Peanuts	1
Innovation Lab	Innovation Lab for Sorghum and Millet	1
Innovation Lab	Innovation Lab for Sustainable Intensification	1

Organization Type	Organization/Office Name	Number Interviewed
Innovation Lab	Monsanto	1
Agricultural Research Institution/Fund	African Agriculture Technology Fund (AATF)	1
Agricultural Research Institution/Fund	Arcadia Biosciences	1
Agricultural Research Institution/Fund	Association of Public Land Grant Universities	1
Agricultural Research Institution/Fund	Australian Center for International Agricultural Research	1
Agricultural Research Institution/Fund	CIMMYT	2
Agricultural Research Institution/Fund	IFPRI	1
Donor/Multilateral	Bill and Melinda Gates Foundation	1
Donor/Multilateral	New Alliance	1
Donor/Multilateral	World Bank/CAADP Multidonor Trust Fund	1
Donor/Multilateral	World Bank/CGIAR Fund	1
Donor/Multilateral	World Bank/GAFSP Fund	1
Implementing Partner	Fintrac	1
Implementing Partner	SPRING	2

Document (Blue = Initiative Level; Yellow= Focus and Aligned Countries; Green = Fieldwork Countries Only)	Overall # of Docs	FY11	FY12	FY13	FY14	FY15	Countries Reviewed	Years Reviewed	Ghana	Bangladesh	Guatemala	Uganda	Malawi	Relevant RQs
FTF Results Framework (overall)	1													1, 10,
FTF Guide	1													1, 3a, 4, 5, 6, 9, 10
FTF MEL Q&A	1													3a, 12
FTF Policy Guide	1													3a, 11
FTF Gender Guideline	1													5
FTF Research Strategy	1													9
FTF Guidance on Integrating Climate Smart Agriculture	1													1
FTF Indicator Handbook	1													2, 4, 10, 12
FTF Guidance Series on HICD	1													4
WEAI Baseline Report	1													5
FTF Understanding and Applying Primary Nutrition Pathways and Principals	1													
FTF Global Landscape Analysis Report on Nutrition	1													6
Evaluation Synthesis of FTF Learning Agenda Evaluations	1													5, 6
FTF Learning Agenda	1													1, 3a, 5, 12
ARP_Progam Area Reviews	5													12
ARP_Program Area Evaluation Reports	9													4, 8, 9
ARP_FISC Program Area Fact Sheets	7													4, 9
BFS Portfolio Reviews	32	4	4	11	52	28		FY2013	1					1, 3, 4, 8, 9, 10, 11, 12
New Alliance Documents (frameworks and reports)	13													8, 10

Document (Blue = Initiative Level; Yellow = Focus and Aligned Countries; Green = Fieldwork Countries Only)	Overall # of Docs	FY11	FY12	FY13	FY14	FY15	Countries Reviewed	Years Reviewed	Ghana	Bangladesh	Guatemala	Uganda	Malawi	Relevant RQs
Multi-Year Strategy (MYS) document	29								1	1	1	1	1	1, 3a, 3b, 4, 6, 7, 8, 11
Annual Focus Country Portfolio Reviews	83		30	25	27	1			3	3	3	3	3	1, 3a, 3b, 4, 7, 11
Ag/Nutrition GLEE Landscapes	19								1	1	1	1	1	
Country Investment Plans (CIPs)	46								1	1	1	1	1	
FTF Cost Benefit Analyses	25								1	1	1	1	1	
Policy Matrices	21								1	1	1	1	1	1, 2, 11
Official Strategy Change Memos	12											1	3	1, 3b, 3c
Baseline PBS Reports from ZOIs	12								1		1	1	1	3b, 3c
Interim PBS Reports from ZOIs	1								1					3b, 3c
Regional/Country-Level Evaluation Reports	12									1			1	3b, 3c
ARP Country Programming Summaries	25								1	1	1	1	1	4, 8, 9
Country Implementation Plan (CIP)	5								1	1	1	1	1	3a, 3c, 7
Project Appraisal Documents (PAD)	10								6	1	1	1	1	3a, 5, 6
FTF portfolio and activity descriptions/fact sheets/success stories	28								12	2	1		13	3a
Activity PMPs	7								2			1	4	3b,
CAADP Plans	0								N/A	N/A				3a, 3c
CAADP Annual Implementation Reports	0								N/A	N/A				3c, 8
CIP Annual Reports	0													3c, 7
Activity Annual Reports (as applicable to ZOI)	37								9	7		7	14	3a, 3c, 5

Document (Blue = Initiative Level; Yellow= Focus and Aligned Countries; Green = Fieldwork Countries Only)	Overall # of Docs	FY11	FY12	FY13	FY14	FY15	Countries Reviewed	Years Reviewed	Ghana	Bangladesh	Guatemala	Uganda	Malawi	Relevant RQs
Activity Evaluation Reports	6								2	1		1	2	1, 3a, 3b, 5, 6
Gender Analysis/Assessment/WEAI reports	4								1	2			1	6

Name	Lee Robert Briggs
Title	Evaluation Team Leader
Organization	Dexis Consulting Group
Evaluation Position?	**X** Team Leader ☐ Team member
Evaluation Award Number *(contract or other instrument)*	AID-OAA-I-15-00019/ AID-OAA-TO-16-00003
USAID Project(s) Evaluated *(Include project name(s), implementer name(s) and award number(s), if applicable)*	Feed the Future Global Performance Evaluation, Dexis Consulting Group
I have real or potential conflicts of interest to disclose.	☐ Yes **X** No
If yes answered above, I disclose the following facts: *Real or potential conflicts of interest may include, but are not limited to:* *1. Close family member who is an employee of the USAID operating unit managing the project(s) being evaluated or the implementing organization(s) whose project(s) are being evaluated.* *2. Financial interest that is direct, or is significant though indirect, in the implementing organization(s) whose projects are being evaluated or in the outcome of the evaluation.* *3. Current or previous direct or significant though indirect experience with the project(s) being evaluated, including involvement in the project design or previous iterations of the project.* *4. Current or previous work experience or seeking employment with the USAID operating unit managing the evaluation or the implementing organization(s) whose project(s) are being evaluated.* *5. Current or previous work experience with an organization that may be seen as an industry competitor with the implementing organization(s) whose project(s) are being evaluated.* *6. Preconceived ideas toward individuals, groups, organizations, or objectives of the*	

| *particular projects and organizations being evaluated that could bias the evaluation.* | |

I certify (1) that I have completed this disclosure form fully and to the best of my ability and (2) that I will update this disclosure form promptly if relevant circumstances change. If I gain access to proprietary information of other companies, then I agree to protect their information from unauthorized use or disclosure for as long as it remains proprietary and refrain from using the information for any purpose other than that for which it was furnished.

Signature	
Date	August 9, 2016

Name	Patricia J Vondal
Title	Senior Evaluation Specialist
Organization	Independent Consultant for Dexis
Evaluation Position?	☐ Team Leader ✓ Team member
Evaluation Award Number (contract or other instrument)	AID-OAA-I-15-00019/ AID-OAA-TO-16-00003
USAID Project(s) Evaluated (Include project name(s), implementer name(s) and award number(s), if applicable)	Feed the Future Global Performance Evaluation, Dexis Consulting Group
I have real or potential conflicts of interest to disclose.	☐ Yes ✓ No
If yes answered above, I disclose the following facts: Real or potential conflicts of interest may include, but are not limited to: 1. Close family member who is an employee of the USAID operating unit managing the project(s) being evaluated or the implementing organization(s) whose project(s) are being evaluated. 2. Financial interest that is direct, or is significant though indirect, in the implementing organization(s) whose projects are being evaluated or in the outcome of the evaluation. 3. Current or previous direct or significant though indirect experience with the project(s) being evaluated, including involvement in the project design or previous iterations of the project. 4. Current or previous work experience or seeking employment with the USAID operating unit managing the evaluation or the implementing organization(s) whose project(s) are being evaluated. 5. Current or previous work experience with an organization that may be seen as an industry competitor with the implementing organization(s) whose project(s) are being evaluated. 6. Preconceived ideas toward individuals, groups, organizations, or objectives of the particular projects and organizations being evaluated that could bias the evaluation.	

I certify (1) that I have completed this disclosure form fully and to the best of my ability and (2) that I will update this disclosure form promptly if relevant circumstances change. If I gain access to proprietary information of other companies, then I agree to protect their information from unauthorized use or disclosure for as long as it remains proprietary and refrain from using the information for any purpose other than that for which it was furnished.

Signature	
Date	July 28, 2016

Name	Andrew Michael Maxey
Title	Senior Agriculture Advisor
Organization	Dexis Consulting
Evaluation Position?	☐ Team Leader X Team member
Evaluation Award Number *(contract or other instrument)*	AID-OAA-I-15-00019/ AID-OAA-TO-16-00003
USAID Project(s) Evaluated *(Include project name(s), implementer name(s) and award number(s), if applicable)*	Feed the Future Global Performance Evaluation, Dexis Consulting Group
I have real or potential conflicts of interest to disclose.	Yes X No
If yes answered above, I disclose the following facts: *Real or potential conflicts of interest may include, but are not limited to:* 7. *Close family member who is an employee of the USAID operating unit managing the project(s) being evaluated or the implementing organization(s) whose project(s) are being evaluated.* 8. *Financial interest that is direct, or is significant though indirect, in the implementing organization(s) whose projects are being evaluated or in the outcome of the evaluation.* 9. *Current or previous direct or significant though indirect experience with the project(s) being evaluated, including involvement in the project design or previous iterations of the project.* 10. *Current or previous work experience or seeking employment with the USAID operating unit managing the evaluation or the implementing organization(s) whose project(s) are being evaluated.* 11. *Current or previous work experience with an organization that may be seen as an industry competitor with the implementing organization(s) whose project(s) are being evaluated.* 12. *Preconceived ideas toward individuals, groups, organizations, or objectives of the particular projects and organizations being evaluated that could bias the evaluation.*	I have no conflict of interest issue.

I certify (1) that I have completed this disclosure form fully and to the best of my ability and (2) that I will update this disclosure form promptly if relevant circumstances change. If I gain access to proprietary information of other companies, then I agree to protect their information from unauthorized use or disclosure for as long as it remains proprietary and refrain from using the information for any purpose other than that for which it was furnished.

Signature	*(signature)*
Date	August 31, 2016

Name	William Fiebig
Title	Senior Technical Advisor
Organization	Dexis Consulting Group
Evaluation Position?	☐ Team Leader ☒ Team member
Evaluation Award Number (contract or other instrument)	AID-OAA-I-15-00019/ AID-OAA-TO-16-00003
USAID Project(s) Evaluated (Include project name(s), implementer name(s) and award number(s), if applicable)	Feed the Future Global Performance Evaluation, Dexis Consulting Group
I have real or potential conflicts of interest to disclose.	☐ Yes ☒ No
If yes answered above, I disclose the following facts: Real or potential conflicts of interest may include, but are not limited to: 1. Close family member who is an employee of the USAID operating unit managing the project(s) being evaluated or the implementing organization(s) whose project(s) are being evaluated. 2. Financial interest that is direct, or is significant though indirect, in the implementing organization(s) whose projects are being evaluated or in the outcome of the evaluation. 3. Current or previous direct or significant though indirect experience with the project(s) being evaluated, including involvement in the project design or previous iterations of the project. 4. Current or previous work experience or seeking employment with the USAID operating unit managing the evaluation or the implementing organization(s) whose project(s) are being evaluated. 5. Current or previous work experience with an organization that may be seen as an industry competitor with the implementing organization(s) whose project(s) are being evaluated. 6. Preconceived ideas toward individuals, groups, organizations, or objectives of the particular projects and organizations being evaluated that could bias the evaluation.	

I certify (1) that I have completed this disclosure form fully and to the best of my ability and (2) that I will update this disclosure form promptly if relevant circumstances change. If I gain access to proprietary information of other companies, then I agree to protect their information from unauthorized use or disclosure for as long as it remains proprietary and refrain from using the information for any purpose other than that for which it was furnished.

Signature	*Wm Feiberg*
Date	*August 16, 2016*

Name	Allyson Bear
Title	Senior Technical Advisor
Organization	Dexis
Evaluation Position?	☐ Team Leader ■ Team member
Evaluation Award Number (contract or other instrument)	AID-OAA-I-15-00019/ AID-OAA-TO-16-00003
USAID Project(s) Evaluated (Include project name(s), implementer name(s) and award number(s), if applicable)	Feed the Future Global Performance Evaluation, Dexis Consulting Group
I have real or potential conflicts of interest to disclose.	■ Yes ☐ No
If yes answered above, I disclose the following facts: Real or potential conflicts of interest may include, but are not limited to: 1. Close family member who is an employee of the USAID operating unit managing the project(s) being evaluated or the implementing organization(s) whose project(s) are being evaluated. 2. Financial interest that is direct, or is significant though indirect, in the implementing organization(s) whose projects are being evaluated or in the outcome of the evaluation. 3. Current or previous direct or significant though indirect experience with the project(s) being evaluated, including involvement in the project design or previous iterations of the project. 4. Current or previous work experience or seeking employment with the USAID operating unit managing the evaluation or the implementing organization(s) whose project(s) are being evaluated. 5. Current or previous work experience with an organization that may be seen as an industry competitor with the implementing organization(s) whose project(s) are being evaluated. 6. Preconceived ideas toward individuals, groups, organizations, or objectives of the particular projects and organizations being evaluated that could bias the evaluation.	I resigned from USAID in 8/2015 from my position as an FSO Health Officer. While employed with USAID I oversaw elements of strategy formulation, design, and implementation of some FTF activities in Mali and Bangladesh. In April 2016 I signed a PSC contract with USAID/Global Health Bureau. The nature of my work under this contract does not have any relationship, perceived or real, with activities conducted under FTF. Work under this contract did not start until July, and was limited to award management of an GH bureau cooperative agreement for the duration of the FTF evaluation. The subject award did not receive any FTF funding. All of these relationships were disclosed in real time, and determined not to be real conflicts of interest for the purpose of this contract.

I certify (1) that I have completed this disclosure form fully and to the best of my ability and (2) that I will update this disclosure form promptly if relevant circumstances change. If I gain access to proprietary information of other companies, then I agree to protect their information from unauthorized use or disclosure for as long as it remains proprietary and refrain from using the information for any purpose other than that for which it was furnished.

Signature	
Date	9/19/2016

Name	Lauren Rosapep
Title	Senior Monitoring & Evaluation Specialist
Organization	Dexis Consulting Group
Evaluation Position?	☐ Team Leader ☒ Team member
Evaluation Award Number *(contract or other instrument)*	AID-OAA-I-15-00019/ AID-OAA-TO-16-00003
USAID Project(s) Evaluated *(include project name(s), implementer name(s) and award number(s), if applicable)*	Feed the Future Global Performance Evaluation, Dexis Consulting Group
I have real or potential conflicts of interest to disclose.	☐ Yes ☒ No
If yes answered above, I disclose the following facts: *Real or potential conflicts of interest may include, but are not limited to:* *1. Close family member who is an employee of the USAID operating unit managing the project(s) being evaluated or the implementing organization(s) whose project(s) are being evaluated.* *2. Financial interest that is direct, or is significant though indirect, in the implementing organization(s) whose projects are being evaluated or in the outcome of the evaluation.* *3. Current or previous direct or significant though indirect experience with the project(s) being evaluated, including involvement in the project design or previous iterations of the project.* *4. Current or previous work experience or seeking employment with the USAID operating unit managing the evaluation or the implementing organization(s) whose project(s) are being evaluated.* *5. Current or previous work experience with an organization that may be seen as an industry competitor with the implementing organization(s) whose project(s) are being evaluated.* *6. Preconceived ideas toward individuals, groups, organizations, or objectives of the particular projects and organizations being evaluated that could bias the evaluation.*	

I certify (1) that I have completed this disclosure form fully and to the best of my ability and (2) that I will update this disclosure form promptly if relevant circumstances change. If I gain access to proprietary information of other companies, then I agree to protect their information from unauthorized use or disclosure for as long as it remains proprietary and refrain from using the information for any purpose other than that for which it was furnished.

Signature	
Date	July 27, 2016

Name	Charu Vijayakumar
Title	M&E Specialist
Organization	Dexis Consulting Group
Evaluation Position?	☐ Team Leader ■ Team member
Evaluation Award Number *(contract or other instrument)*	AID-OAA-I-15-00019/ AID-OAA-TO-16-00003
USAID Project(s) Evaluated *(Include project name(s), implementer name(s) and award number(s), if applicable)*	Feed the Future Global Performance Evaluation, Dexis Consulting Group
I have real or potential conflicts of interest to disclose.	☐ Yes ■ No
If yes answered above, I disclose the following facts: *Real or potential conflicts of interest may include, but are not limited to:* 1. *Close family member who is an employee of the USAID operating unit managing the project(s) being evaluated or the implementing organization(s) whose project(s) are being evaluated.* 2. *Financial interest that is direct, or is significant though indirect, in the implementing organization(s) whose projects are being evaluated or in the outcome of the evaluation.* 3. *Current or previous direct or significant though indirect experience with the project(s) being evaluated, including involvement in the project design or previous iterations of the project.* 4. *Current or previous work experience or seeking employment with the USAID operating unit managing the evaluation or the implementing organization(s) whose project(s) are being evaluated.* 5. *Current or previous work experience with an organization that may be seen as an industry competitor with the implementing organization(s) whose project(s) are being evaluated.* 6. *Preconceived ideas toward individuals, groups, organizations, or objectives of the particular projects and organizations being evaluated that could bias the evaluation.*	

I certify (1) that I have completed this disclosure form fully and to the best of my ability and (2) that I will update this disclosure form promptly if relevant circumstances change. If I gain access to proprietary information of other companies, then I agree to protect their information from unauthorized use or disclosure for as long as it remains proprietary and refrain from using the information for any purpose other than that for which it was furnished.

Signature	
Date	7 / 27 / 16

Name	Amun Nadeem
Title	
Organization	Dexis Consulting Group
Evaluation Position?	Team Leader **X**Team member
Evaluation Award Number *(contract or other instrument)*	AID-OAA-I-15-00019/ AID-OAA-TO-16-00003
USAID Project(s) Evaluated *(Include project name(s), implementer name(s) and award number(s), if applicable)*	Feed the Future Global Performance Evaluation, Dexis Consulting Group
I have real or potential conflicts of interest to disclose.	Yes **X** No
If yes answered above, I disclose the following facts: *Real or potential conflicts of interest may include, but are not limited to:* 13. *Close family member who is an employee of the USAID operating unit managing the project(s) being evaluated or the implementing organization(s) whose project(s) are being evaluated.* 14. *Financial interest that is direct, or is significant though indirect, in the implementing organization(s) whose projects are being evaluated or in the outcome of the evaluation.* 15. *Current or previous direct or significant though indirect experience with the project(s) being evaluated, including involvement in the project design or previous iterations of the project.* 16. *Current or previous work experience or seeking employment with the USAID operating unit managing the evaluation or the implementing organization(s) whose project(s) are being evaluated.* 17. *Current or previous work experience with an organization that may be seen as an industry competitor with the implementing organization(s) whose project(s) are being evaluated.* 18. *Preconceived ideas toward individuals, groups, organizations, or objectives of the particular projects and organizations being evaluated that could bias the evaluation.*	

I certify (1) that I have completed this disclosure form fully and to the best of my ability and (2) that I will update this disclosure form promptly if relevant circumstances change. If I gain access to proprietary information of other companies, then I agree to protect their information from unauthorized use or disclosure for as long as it remains proprietary and refrain from using the information for any purpose other than that for which it was furnished.

Signature	
Date	09/19/16

Table A: PBS Results[1]

COUNTRY	PREVELANCE OF POVERTY[2]			PREVELANCE OF STUNTING[3]		
	Baseline Result	Interim Result	Difference	Baseline Result	Interim Result	Difference
Bangladesh	**40.50%**	**34.01%**	**-16.02%**	**36.90%**	**32.30%**	**-12.47%**
Cambodia	**11.70%**	**8.68%**	**-25.81%**	**43.95%**	**33.70%**	**-23.32%**
Ethiopia	**39.90%**	**35.00%**	**-12.28%**	49.20%	47.10%	-4.27%
Ghana	**22.20%**	**19.60%**	**-11.71%**	**36.10%**	**29.90%**	**-17.17%**
Guatemala	**5.90%**	**4.28%**	**-27.46%**	**67.40%**	**63.32%**	**-6.05%**
Honduras	45.80%	45.80%	0.00%	**38.30%**	**26.10%**	**-31.85%**
Kenya (HR/SA)	44.70%	46.92%	4.97%	**35.10%**	**20.93%**	**-40.37%**
Kenya (northern)	61.90%	58.50%	-5.49%	27.60%	26.30%	-4.71%
Liberia	**49.40%**	**39.80%**	**-19.43%**	43.10%	34.30%	-20.42%
Malawi	**66.70%**	**54.50%**	**-18.29%**	**49.20%**	**42.30%**	**-14.02%**
Mozambique	62.00%	66.50%	7.26%	51.60%	51.80%	0.39%
Nepal	**32.50%**	**20.90%**	**-35.69%**	45.20%	47.00%	3.98%
Rwanda	**67.00%**	**62.00%**	**-7.46%**	**46.30%**	**39.70%**	**-14.25%**
Senegal	34.30%	40.50%	18.08%	23.10%	25.80%	11.69%
Tajikistan	8.80%	10.40%	18.18%	30.70%	29.30%	-4.56%
Tanzania	**37.20%**	**28.20%**	**-24.19%**	34.70%	37.70%	8.65%
Uganda	32.90%	32.10%	-2.43%	33.00%	29.20%	-11.52%
Zambia	**88.00%**	**80.90%**	**-8.07%**	45.50%	38.40%	-15.60%

[1] Lines that are bolded and in color indicate statistically significant change. Remaining lines are either not statistically significant or are inconclusive without further analysis.

[2] Percent of people living on less than $1.25/day

[3] Prevalence of stunted children under five years of age

Table B: Value Chain Summary Table

Country	Zone of Influence	Target Population	Country Priorities	Value Chains and Rationale
Bangladesh	• High potential of AG growth (additional crop/yr) • High poverty rate • Climate variability and susceptible to cyclones and natural disasters • High stunting rate • Farmer breadbasket • Overlap Title II and GH • Historically under-supported area • Reclaim previous breadbasket (now saline due to climate change	• Poor w/>$2/day, land, market links • Ultra poor w/<$1/day, landless, isolated	• Sustainable climate change response • Improved water management and infrastructure for irrigation • Supply and sustainable use of inputs • Fishery development • Livestock development • Access to markets • Increased added value • Increased farm income	**Rice** – staple, few distortions, stagnant productivity. **Maize** – can rotate with rice for second crop, use for chicken and fish feed, production is rising quickly **Fish** – ideal habitat, source of income, most important animal protein
Cambodia	• Very high poverty rates and food insecurity • High child malnutrition • High soil fertility • 80% of inland fisheries	• Food insecure • Women	• Increased food availability from own AG and livestock production • Increased food access through increased income • Improved food use and utilization • Improved social safety nets and capacity to cope with risks • Improved policy environment	**Rice** – Staple, source of income **Horticulture** – Women's income from production, processing and marketing. Improved availability and consumption of diverse and nutrient rich food. Reduce reliance on imports. **Fish** – Basic protein source, complements rice production cycle (off season production)
Ethiopia	• Hungry • Pastoral • Productive	• Hungry area - poverty and chronic and acute malnutrition, vulnerability • Pastoral area – poverty, malnutrition, vulnerability, repeated crises	• Only documentation on USAID/Ethiopia agreements, not Ethiopia policy per se. • Focus on smallholder growth potential, nutrition, job creation, adding value, women and	**Dairy** – Economic growth, nutrition, job creation for women. To a lesser extent, links to vulnerable populations **Meat** – Economic growth, nutrition, job creation for women. To a lesser extent,

Country	Zone of Influence	Target Population	Country Priorities	Value Chains and Rationale
		• Productive area – poverty, lack of service and market access, vulnerability, degraded resources	reducing vulnerability, especially to agro-climatic shocks.	links to vulnerable populations **Maize** – Economic growth, job creation for women, links to vulnerable populations. To a lesser extent nutrition. **Wheat** – Economic growth, job creation for women, links to vulnerable populations. To a lesser extent, nutrition. **Honey** – Economic growth, job creation for women. **Coffee** – Job creation for women. To a lesser extent, economic growth
Ghana	• Northern provinces • Select Coastal fishing areas	• Poverty • Remoteness • Historically ignored areas • Government interest	• Government commitment to northern provinces • Agriculture and value chain development • Poverty alleviation	**Rice** – Staple, active processors **Soy** – Rotational copping w/maize, high potential, nutrition, staple **Maize** – Staple food, active processors **Marine Fisheries** – Availability of protein and employment
Guatemala	Western Highlands based on: • High poverty rates • High chronic malnutrition • Indigenous populations • Historically marginalized area	• Poor farmers • Households with children under 2	• Inclusive country-led food security planning • Integrated and sustainable coordination and implementation to reduce the risks to nutrition and food security • Western Highlands	**Coffee** – incomes, employment **Horticulture (snow peas and French beans for US/EU markets)**– income, nutrition **Handicrafts** – women's income, especially those who are extremely poor
Haiti	• Watersheds prioritized by government • AG potential • # of beneficiaries • Distance to market • Availability of rural credit	• Food insecure populations • Vulnerable populations, especially to agro-climatic and economic factors	• AG growth • Development of rural areas • Watershed management • Development of competitive value chains • Increased research and education,	**Mango** – Highest export potential, trees for hillside stability **Cocoa** – Internal market demand increasing, trees for hillside stability **Coffee** – Export potential, trees for hillside stability

Country	Zone of Influence	Target Population	Country Priorities	Value Chains and Rationale
			services and land tenure • Food insecurity	
Honduras	West: • Reduce transactions costs • Poorest municipalities • Maximize MDG achievement	• Farmers • Farmer organizations • Private-sector actors • Rural unemployed	• Improved food security • Market-led agriculture growth and poverty alleviation • Market access to historically remote and less accessible areas.	**Vegetables** – Diverse, year-round production, food, income **Fruit** – Diverse, year-round production, food, income **Coffee** – Unrealized potential, high potential, smallholder, specialty product qualifications
Kenya	HRI and SA2 • Highest poverty/number of poor • Staple food production • Ethnic diversity	• Greatest AG output potential • Poverty density, especially female HOH • Lowest incomes in AG areas • Child malnutrition • For one area, ethnic diversity	• Shift toward irrigation • Create a commercial and modern AG sector • Improve competitiveness	**Dairy** – High income potential, diversification, nutrition **Horticulture** – High income potential, diversification, market dominated by women. **Maize (drought resistant)** – Greatest share of diet and crop income, subsistence need precedes investment in other crops **Drought-tolerant grains (millet, sorghum and cassava** – **Pulses** – Protein, associated crop for lean season, women's crop
Liberia	Lofa, Nimba, Grand Bassa, Montserrado and Margibi Counties: • Greatest population • Most farmers • Greatest AG potential • Population below the poverty line • Situated along the main development corridors	• Women • Youth	• Focus on women and youth. • Environmental and forest protection • Value chain or market linkages • Pre and post harvesting losses and processing (adding value) and fortification	**Rice** – Basic food, women's income **Cassava** – Food, women's crop, fortification **Goats** – Women's farm enterprise, production for consumption and market **Vegetables** – Women's traditional in production and marketing. Youth peri-urban gardens.
Malawi	Central and Southern Regions • Highest poverty	• Women • Producers of specific crops	• Food security • Reduce poverty • Risk management	**Dairy** – High potential, local and export markets, women's participation

Country	Zone of Influence	Target Population	Country Priorities	Value Chains and Rationale
	• Untapped dairy production • Legume linkages to animal sector • Highest rates of under nutrition	and dairy (enterprise focus)	• Market development • Land and water management • Institution strengthening	**Legumes (soy, pigeon pea and groundnuts)** – High potential, high demand from local and export markets, women's crop and income, nutrition and diversification away from maize, demand for feed, jobs.
Mali	Sikasso – Greatest AG productivity Mopti – Sorghum, rice, millet and cattle Segou – Just nutrition Timbuktu – Sorghum and rice	• Smallholders	• Rice production • Sorghum/Millet production • Maize production • Horticulture production • Livestock production • Reduce poverty • Improve nutrition • Reduce vulnerability • Boost economic growth	**Rice** – Large number of beneficiaries, market demand, reduced poverty and vulnerability, GOM priority, multiplier effects, growth potential. **Sorghum/Millet** – Large number of beneficiaries, market demand, reduced poverty and vulnerability, GOM priority, multiplier effects, some growth potential. **Livestock** - Large number of beneficiaries, market demand, reduced poverty and vulnerability, GOM priority, multiplier effects, growth potential, nutrition
Mozambique	• Poverty • Under nutrition • Population size • # of farmers • Potential impact • Complementary investments • Zambezie and Nampula trade corridors	• Smallholders • Women	• Poverty reduction • Improved food security • Regional trade • Integration of nutrition into AG	**Oilseeds (soy, sesame, groundnuts)** – Increase incomes, demand, nutrition, female-headed households participate in production. **Cashews** – Public-private partnership, increase incomes **Fruit** – Income potential, export options, private sector investment, micronutrients/nutrition.
Nepal	Western Terai and Hills: • Greatest potential • Transport networks • Greatest # of poor	• Vulnerable groups – women, disadvantaged and conflict-affected youth	• Rice • Maize • Bananas • Spices • Vegetables • Pulses	**Rice** – High unmet demand, production potential, government priority, nutrition, smallholders production, increase

Country	Zone of Influence	Target Population	Country Priorities	Value Chains and Rationale
	• Greatest # of malnourished	• Ethnic, linguistic and religious groups	• Potato	productivity of staples to promote diversity, e.g., vegetables **Maize** – High unmet demand, production potential, government priority, nutrition, smallholder production, increase productivity of staples to promote diversity, e.g., vegetables **Pulses** – High unmet demand, production potential, government priority, nutrition, protein smallholder production **Vegetables** – Unmet demand, production potential, government priority, high value, nutrition, smallholder production, complement to other crops, competitiveness
Rwanda	Whole country	• Smallholders • Women	• Crop intensification – wide range of crops including the VC selected	**Beans** – Poverty elasticity, # of HH, competiveness, government priority **Maize** – Poverty elasticity, # of HH, government priority **Soy** – Government priority (as subset of beans), nutrition, food security, intercropping with and providing nitrogen to maize production. **Dairy** – US previous experience, Increasing demand for soy **Coffee** – High-value export **Pyrethrum** – Poverty elasticity, US previous experience, competitiveness
Senegal	• Senegal River Valley – Source of irrigated rice, environment,	• Producers of key cereals • Women		**Rice** – 45% of diet, yields advantage within WA region,

Country	Zone of Influence	Target Population	Country Priorities	Value Chains and Rationale
	supports government priorities • Southern Forest Zone- Potential breadbasket, high multiplier effects, protein source			# of farmers, women role in the value chain. **Maize** – Many producers, growing demand poultry and livestock feed, culinary powder, baby cereal market (fortified with cowpeas and groundnuts) **Millet** – Most cultivated crop, current donor support, unmet demand, small processers are mostly women. **Fisheries** – Primary export, big employer, protein, need for greater governance of resource
Tajikistan	Khatlon Province: • High rates of malnutrition • High rates of poverty • High agricultural potential • Borders Afghanistan and Uzbekistan	• Household producers • Small-scale commercial producers		**Fruits** – Income and growth potential, nutritional value, gardens are common, women's involvement in production and marketing, external market **Vegetables** – Income and growth potential, nutritional value, gardens are common, women's involvement in production and marketing, external market
Tanzania	• Moderate to high levels of food insecurity and poverty combined with high potential for growth • Proximity to transport corridors and markets • Lack of alternative donor investment • Appropriate water and climatic conditions for selected VCs	• Productive poor • Women	• Food security • SAGCOT growth corridor • Private-sector led AG growth	**Rice** – Good potential for economic growth and multiplier effects (private-sector investment and jobs) through agro-processing, important income and staple crop, potential synergy with horticulture, collaboration with other donors. **Maize** – Greater participation of small-scale millers and poor households, nutrition via fortification, increase in overall food

Country	Zone of Influence	Target Population	Country Priorities	Value Chains and Rationale
	• Opportunity to impact productive poor • Ability to scale high growth impacts			supply, local procurement option for food assistance **Horticulture** – Nutrition, women's participation, rotational cropping with irrigated rice, private-sector agro-processing investments through SAGCOT
Uganda	• 47 districts in southwest and north with high levels of poverty and under nutrition (stunting and wasting), increasing population, opportunities to integrate and link to other FTF programs • 7 districts in Karamoja – area of great need and continuing conflict, subject to frequent droughts.	• Smallholders • Vulnerable women • Vulnerable children	• Maize • Coffee • Beans • Fish • Dairy • Cattle • Tea • Cassava • Poultry • Banana	**Maize** – Strong WFP and regional market for smallholders, grown by 2/3 of population, unmet demand, regional shortfalls, untapped potential **Beans** – Nutrition staple, grown by 2/3 of population, shares post harvest infrastructure with maize, multiplier effects with maize production **Coffee** – Top AG export, major GDP contributor, grown by 1/3 of population, demand outstrips demand, high-end specialized coffee niche possibilities **Livestock** – Karamoja. Primary food security and livelihood strategy, source or affected by conflict.
Zambia	Eastern Province and Selected peri-urban districts of Lusaka/Central: • Number of smallholders • # of people living in poverty • # of underweight children • Potential commercialization of high-priority staple food crops	• Poor smallholders • Women	• Pro-Poor economic growth • Macroeconomic stability • Reduce poverty • Improve income distribution • Gender inclusion • Eastern Province and Lusaka area	**Oilseeds and legumes** – Potential for productivity growth, nutrition, women play a prominent role in production, marketing and trade **Maize** – Number of producers, potential for productivity growth, Female headed households have on average .5 ha less than males **Horticulture** – Number of producers, potential for

Country	Zone of Influence	Target Population	Country Priorities	Value Chains and Rationale
	• SACGOT			productivity growth, low-labor requirement

U.S. Agency for International Development
1300 Pennsylvania Avenue, NW
Washington, DC 20523

www.ingramcontent.com/pod-product-compliance
Lightning Source LLC
Chambersburg PA
CBHW081348280526
45788CB00009B/2804